Murphy's Laws
of **COMBAT**

The American Warrior's Guide
to *Staying Alive* in Battle

Marion F. Sturkey

Heritage Press International

Murphy's Laws of Combat

Library of Congress Control Number: 2003101044

ISBN: 0-9650814-4-3

First Edition

Heritage Press International
204 Jefferson Street
P.O. Box 333
Plum Branch, SC 29845 USA

Manufactured in the United States of America

Acknowledgements

Grateful acknowledgement is extended to the late Capt. Edward A. Murphy Jr. (1917-1987), USAF, "father" of Murphy's Law. In 1949, Capt. Murphy first uttered the prophetic statement which became the basis for this perpetual thorn in the foot of humanity. Since that time Murphy's Law has grown, mutated, expanded, and achieved immortality in the popular imagination of all mankind.

Further, grateful acknowledgement is extended to each American Patriot who has served in the Armed Forces of the United States of America. Through selfless sacrifices for brothers-in-arms, they have preserved our great nation for generations yet to come.

Further, grateful acknowledgement is extended to the United States Marine Corps Recruiting Command for assistance in regard to the USMC Recruiting Poster images which are depicted on the front and rear cover of this book.

Further, grateful acknowledgement is extended to the owners of Leeson Photography for assistance in regard to the photograph (later computer-enhanced) depicted on the rear cover of this book.

Table of Contents

PART ONE: Murphy's Laws for Civilians

PART TWO: Murphy's Laws of Combat

PART THREE: Heritage of the American Warrior

-- PART ONE --
-- Murphy's Laws for Civilians --

-- PART TWO --
-- Murphy's Laws of Combat --

(continued on next page)

Table of Contents (continued)

-- PART THREE --
-- Heritage of the American Warrior --

-- military books by Marion Sturkey --

BONNIE-SUE: A Marine Corps Helicopter Squadron in Vietnam:
(first published in 1996) Professional, 21 photographs, 4 maps, 509
pages. A timeless classic, usually considered the definitive work
on Marine Corps helicopter warfare in Vietnam. Yet, the book
soars high above the mud of war. The author blends emotion,
detail, and grim realism; he breathes life into a daily struggle for
survival. Against the backdrop of the turbulent 1960's era,
BONNIE-SUE' evolves into a riveting true saga of commitment and
sacrifice, love and brotherhood. No profanity.

Warrior Culture of the U.S. Marines: (first published in 2002) 15
photographs, 207 pages. Gung-ho, <u>Politically In-Correct</u> and proud
of it! The book extolls the legendary warrior ethos of the U.S.
Marines, the modern-day American Samurai. It's all here: USMC
quotations, Tun Tavern, the creeds, the War Memorial, the
Commandants, axioms for warriors, and patriot dreams. Also,
blood chit, blood stripe, Corps Values (and much more), plus the
ultimate collection of USMC satire. No profanity.

Murphy's Laws of Combat: (first published in 2003) A walk on
the humorous side of military life. Military satire for all branches
of the U.S. Armed Forces. Hundreds upon hundreds of spirited,
up-beat, and *tongue-in-cheek* Combat Laws, Principles, and
Axioms. Plus, the Warrior's Rules of Sex & Seduction. Also,
historic military quotations, battle legacy, and somber Reflections
on Combat from America's military elite. This is the book for
warriors (or warrior wannabes), young and old, who enjoy a good
laugh -- usually at themselves. No profanity.

Heritage Press International
204 Jefferson Street
P.O. Box 333
Plum Branch, SC 29845

Phone:	864-443-5081
Fax:	864-443-5572
E-mail:	MarionS@wctel.net
Web Site:	www.USMCpress.com

Heads Up!

<u>Military Service Abbreviations</u>: The most frequently referenced Armed Forces are identified by abbreviations:

USA	United States Army
USN	United States Navy
USMC	United States Marine Corps
USAF	United States Air Force
CSA	Confederate States Army
RN	Royal Navy (British)
RAF	Royal Air Force (British)

<u>Civilian Sources</u>: The title, position, occupation, or claim to fame of civilian sources is given when known, for example: (1) U.S. Senator, (2) French military strategist, (3) German philosopher, (4) British Prime Minister, etc.

<u>On Active Duty</u>? With respect to rank and military organization, this book makes no distinction between military warriors on active duty, military retirees, military veterans, military reservists, etc.

<u>Duplications</u>: Quotations from various chapters in this book are *intentionally duplicated* in "Murphy's Military Superlatives" and in Part Three.

Notice!

Politically Impossible!

The content of this book is tailored for the elite and professional American Warriors. **<u>Gender</u>?** **<u>Who knows</u>?** **<u>Who cares</u>?** The reader will find no *politically correct* psycho-babble. There is no "he or she" stupidity or "him or her" childishness. The male pronoun suffices for all gung-ho warriors, both men and women.

Any cowardly communist pinko hand-wringing weakling who is offended by this warrior culture ethos should find something else to read, such as *Floral Arrangements for All Occasions*.

Those who dance are
thought to be quite insane
by those who can not
hear the music.

PART ONE

Murphy's Laws
for
Civilians

The Origin
of
Murphy's Law

Murphy's Law is ***not*** a figment of creative imagination. This timeless truth has existed since time immemorial. Yet, it was not officially named and published until the Twentieth Century.

After World War II, United States aerospace experiments shifted into high gear. U.S. Air Force Project MX-981 used a "rocket sled" test program. On the sled, named the *Sonic Wind*, volunteers explored the G-force limits the human body can withstand.

Capt. Edward A. Murphy Jr. (1917-1987), USAF, a brilliant young Air Force aerospace engineer, worked on these rocket sled experiments at what is now Edwards Air Force Base in California. One sunny morning in 1949, Murphy's staff strapped a hapless volunteer, Maj. John P. Stapp, USAF, into the rocket sled. A technician dutifully attached 16 sensors, called accelerometers, to the sled. Murphy had calculated that Stapp would be subjected to roughly 40 G's for precisely 1.7 seconds.

When all was ready, the rockets ignited with a deafening roar. The sled blasted down the rails, propelled by a white-hot furnace of flame from the rocket. Then the rocket motor died, and the sled screeched to a stop.

Medical aides ran to help Maj. Stapp, who was semiconscious and bleeding from several body orifices. The aides spirited him away for a medical check-up. Murphy's technicians then checked the sled. To their dismay, they found that all of the accelerometers registered zero G-forces. What had gone wrong?

Murphy soon found the problem. The technician who installed the 16 accelerometers had carefully installed each of them -- ***backwards***! Murphy reacted as though struck by lightning. Leaping to his feet, he looked toward Heaven and lamented:

If there are two or more ways to do something, and one of those ways will result in a catastrophe, someone will do it that way!

George Nichols, the project manager, realized that he had heard the ultimate cosmic truth. He wrote Murphy's lamentation in his notebook. As an afterthought, Nichols jotted down an off-the-cuff caption, **"Murphy's Law."**

The next day at a press conference, a revived Maj. Stapp talked with the media. He joked that despite "Murphy's Law" the rocket sled project had a good safety record.

George Nichols and Maj. Stapp had planted the seed of truth. Within weeks the newfound "Murphy's Law" began appearing in aerospace advertisements. Soon it spread to the Flight Safety Foundation, which published an abbreviated version:

If anything *can* go wrong, it *will* go wrong!

Within months Murphy's Law spread to various technology ventures and engineering firms. Soon it migrated onto college campuses and into the business world. It grew and grew, mutating and evolving all the while.

In 1958, Webster's Dictionary included Murphy's Law, bowing to the inherent truth of this perpetual thorn in the foot of humanity. Murphy's Law eventually spanned oceans and cultures, achieving immortality in the popular imagination of all mankind.

> The universal aptitude for ineptitude makes any human accomplishment an incredible miracle.
> [Col. John P. Stapp, USAF; the brave volunteer who survived many a ride in the *Sonic Wind* rocket sled, and whose gallant efforts helped to expand the frontiers of aerospace science]

Murphy's Basic Laws
for
All Mankind

Over the years, Murphy's original laws have evolved to meet the realities of modern hi-tech warfare. Murphy's Laws of Combat offer invaluable insight into a warrior's number one goal in battle: *staying alive*. But before we examine the laws and rules of warfare, we must understand the elementary basics.

Murphy's basic laws govern all human endeavors, military and civilian alike. Historically, these fundamental truths have formed a ball and chain around the foot of progress. Tragically, these laws are constant, there is no appeal, and there is no escape. Therefore, before a warrior delves into the laws which govern the military arts, he must gain an understanding of the bedrock principles which plague all mankind.

Although Edward Murphy passed away in 1987, his philosophy will live forever. Murphy's Law will never die. So in a sense, one could truthfully say that Murphy and his legacy are alive and well. In that context, "Murphy" sets forth his fundamental laws for humanity in three simple categories:

1. Murphy's General Laws
2. Murphy's Technology Laws
3. Murphy's Technological Advice

-- Murphy's General Laws --

If anything *can* go wrong, it *will* go wrong!

If something simply can not go wrong, it will anyway.

Things that go wrong will do so when you least expect it.

If there is an absolutely, positively, worst time for something to go wrong, it will go wrong then.

When two or more things go wrong, they will do so all at once.

If you determine there are four possible ways in which something can go wrong, and circumvent those four, then a fifth way, unprepared for, will develop.

You *never* run out of things that can go wrong.

Of two possible events, only the undesired one will occur.

Any event which would create chaos if it did occur, will occur.

Left to themselves, things go from bad to worse.

Nothing is ever so bad that it can not get worse.

Sooner or later, the worst possible condition will occur.

Things always will get worse before they get better -- and then they will *not* get better.

Things are not usually as bad as they seem. They are worse.

Things get worse under pressure.

Things always get *much* worse at night.

After having gone from bad to worst, the cycle will repeat itself.

Anything that begins well ends badly.

Anything that begins badly ends worse.

There is no limit to how bad things can get.

Two wrongs are only the beginning.

Nothing is as easy as it looks.

Anything *may* be possible, but nothing is easy.

Everything takes longer than you think.

Nothing can be done in the allotted time.

Anything is easier to get into than out of.

Nothing is impossible for those who do not have to do it.

You can never merely do *one* thing (whenever you set out to do something, something else always must be done first).

Nature always sides with the hidden flaw.

Unfortunately, the hidden flaw never remains hidden for long.

Yet, if there is a hidden *solution*, it will remain hidden.

Nothing is so simple that it can not be misunderstood.

Each failure further reinforces the failure mind-set.

Tragically, the magnitude of a failure will be *directly* proportional to the need for success.

Nothing succeeds like failure, and when failure rains, it pours.

The most crucial problems have no genuine solutions.

If you think the problem is bad now, just wait until it is solved!

In the unlikely event that there is a correct solution to a problem, it will magnify the problem.

Each problem solved breeds a new and more complex problem.

Even the most complex problems usually have simple and easy to understand wrong answers.

Every person has a unique sure-fire solution that will not work.

The answer to a complex problem may be right, wrong, both, or neither, and all answers are partly right and partly wrong.

The number of seemingly rational hypotheses that can explain any given phenomena is always infinite.

Nothing is devoid of side effects, nothing ever goes away, and there is no free lunch.

The bird in hand is usually dead.

Nothing is as good as it seemed beforehand.

Things that are supposed to happen do not happen (but the most undesired and unexpected thing *will* happen).

Most things, if left to chance, would turn out much better.

Everything depends, and everything breaks down.

Nothing is ever done for the right reason.

There is no such thing as an absolute truth.

Ninety percent of everything is crud.

There is always a way, but it usually will not work.

Most of what you think is right is wrong.

There is always something additional that is wrong.

Those who are not confused are not well informed.

If opportunity knocks, it will be at the least opportune moment.

You get the most of what you need the least.

Variables will never vary, and change is the only constant.

The cream rises and rises and rises -- until it sours.

Those who fail to study history will repeat its errors. Those who do study history will find other ways to err.

-- Murphy's Technology Laws --

Most advanced technology is indistinguishable from magic.

Any sufficiently advanced technology which depends on human reliability is unreliable.

Anticipated events never occur, and if they seem to occur, they never live up to expectations.

Any unexpected sequence of events will be followed by an unexpected sequence of trouble.

If, on an actuarial basis, there is a 50-50 chance that something will go wrong, it will go wrong nine times out of ten.

Once a job is irrevocably screwed up, anything done to try to improve it will only make it worse.

The reliability of any system is *inversely* proportional to the square of its complexity.

If the assumptions are wrong, so are the conclusions.

If a scientific process simply can not go wrong, it will anyway.

In a crisis, if the experts all agree, they are all wrong.

In a crisis, whatever hits the fan is never evenly distributed.

An ounce of applicability is worth a ton of abstract theory.

Sadly, an ounce of image is valued more than a ton of competence.

Nothing is ever right in nature. Therefore, if something looks natural, it is always wrong.

Man will occasionally stumble over the truth. Unfortunately he will usually pick himself up, dust himself off, and continue on as though nothing has happened.

There is always a solution -- neat, plausible, and wrong.

If a complex experiment seemed to work, something went wrong.

If the experiment *really* worked, you used the wrong equipment.

Indecision is the secret key to flexibility.

Logic is a systematic scientific method of coming to the wrong conclusion with confidence.

Most of the time, it is better to be lucky than logical.

Nonetheless, no logical act goes unpunished.

When things go wrong, the urgency of repair work will be *inversely* proportional to the availability of spare parts.

If it *can* be borrowed and broken, it *will* be borrowed and broken.

If a thing can break, it will, but only after the warranty has expired.

If everything seems to be going exactly as planned, you have overlooked something.

If it were not for the last minute, nothing would ever get done.

If there is a possibility of several things going wrong, and only one actually goes wrong, it will be the one that will (1) cause the most damage and (2) cost the most money.

Everything takes more time and more money.

In any process, the probability of a thing happening is *inversely* proportional to its desirability.

Under the most rigorously controlled conditions of pressure, temperature, volume, humidity, time, and sterility, the organism will do as it darn well pleases.

Undetectable errors are infinite in quantity and variety.

Nobody perceives anything with total accuracy.

When a thing is used to its full potential, it will break.

Each falling object will fall in the precise manner necessary to do the most damage.

If only one object falls, it will be the most delicate component.

Eventually, *all* delicate components will be dropped.

Things put together will fall apart sooner or later -- usually sooner.

When things seem to be going well, some idiot will inevitably experiment detrimentally.

In scientific circles, all reasoning consists of searching for arguments to justify believing what you already believe.

Try as you may, you can never tell which way the train went by looking at the tracks.

Creativity varies *inversely* with the number of people planning.

Any system, however complicated, if examined in precisely the right way, will become even more complicated.

Tell a man there are 300 billion stars in the universe, and he will believe you. Tell him the bench has wet paint on it, and he will touch it to make sure.

-- Murphy's Technological Advice --

Do not believe in miracles; *rely* on them.

If at first you do not succeed, you will not *ever* succeed. Destroy all of the evidence that you tried.

If at first you do not succeed, the only way to avoid further failure is to quit trying.

All truly great discoveries are made by mistake.

Any great discovery is more likely to be exploited by the wicked than applied by the virtuous.

After all other options have failed, read the instructions.

If a machine jams, do not force it. Try a bigger hammer.

It usually works better if you plug it in.

The first rule of intelligent tinkering is to save all parts.

If you tinker with something long enough, it will break.

To pick the smartest person, select the one who predicts the project will (1) take too long, (2) cost too much, and (3) fail.

When working on the solution to a complex problem, it is useful to already know the answer.

When you do not know what you are doing, do it neatly.

No experiment is ever a complete and total failure. It always can serve as a bad example.

If a wrong thing is done long enough, it becomes right.

If it can not be expressed numerically, it is a theory, not a fact.

Enough research will support the most ludicrous theory.

Any theory will fit any facts, if you make enough assumptions.

Attempt the impossible and you will *prove* that it is impossible.

The sooner you fall behind, the more time you have to catch up.

If you think you see the light at the end of the tunnel, it often will be the headlight of an oncoming train.

Letting a weasel out of the bag is easier than putting it back in.

If you open a can of worms, the only way you can re-can them is with a bigger and more expensive can.

Lost things will be found in the last place you look (*think* about it).

Luck is an acceptable substitute for competence, but only for those who somehow can be *consistently* lucky.

If the shoe fits, you are not allowing for growth.

When, mathematically, you end up with the wrong answer, try multiplying by the page number.

No matter how hard you try, in life (1) you can not win, (2) you can not break even, and (3) you can not quit.

After all is said and done, more usually has been said than done.

PART TWO

Murphy's Laws of Combat

Murphy's Laws of Combat
for
Infantry

The basic laws of combat never change. Warriors must learn from the fatal mistakes of others. Otherwise, in combat they will not survive long enough to learn how to survive permanently.

Although basic laws of combat do not change, weapons do. In the beginning, combatants used their fists and teeth. Later they graduated to clubs and big rocks. Pretty soon a sharpened stick evolved into a spear. Then a sharpened rock, strapped to a club, became a sophisticated war ax. High-tech stuff!

Swords and shields quickly followed. The long-bow and its arrows came next, and later the mechanized crossbow became an even more lethal and accurate killing machine. Then the Chinese stumbled across gunpowder, and the rest is history.

The modern warrior charges into battle while armed with a dizzying array of guns, mines, rockets, missiles, and electronic smart weapons. He can race overland from one battlefield to the next, protected inside of lethal armored chariots. At his beck and call are flying machines of incredible speed and complexity, which can rain aerial death and destruction down upon the enemy.

Professional warriors, pay attention! Murphy's Laws of Combat for Infantry apply to all warriors. But they are of primary interest to the elite population control specialists, the supremely skilled corps of government assassins, the **Magnificent Grunts**.

Warriors, handed down through the ages, here are your Laws of Combat. These are your time-tested axioms and principles for winning in battle. If **staying alive** is important to you, ignore them at your own peril. Murphy presents these priceless martial art pearls of wisdom in the following six categories:

1. Murphy's Combat Philosophy
2. Murphy's Essential Dozen Rules for Firefights
3. Murphy's Combat Tactics

-- Murphy's Combat Philosophy --

If you are allergic to lead, you would be wise to avoid combat.

In combat, any warrior who does not openly consider himself the best in the game is in the *wrong* game.

War does not decide who is right. War decides who is left.

There is only one overriding rule in warfare -- the winner always gets to make up the rules.

Remember that *diplomacy* is the art of saying "nice doggie" until you can find a bigger rock.

You may be able to win without fighting, and it is preferable. But it also is *harder*, and the enemy may not cooperate.

Sooner or later in life, every warrior has to die. The trick is to die young, as late as possible.

Warriors live a rough life. Only the young die good.

The only warriors fit to live are those who are not afraid to die.

For civilians, to *err* is human, to *forgive* is divine. For warriors in combat, neither is acceptable.

Medals are OK. Having all your warrior brothers alive is better.

In combat, no matter how bad it gets, having all of your body parts intact and functioning makes it a good day.

When you win, nothing hurts!

When you win, you are entitled to the spoils of war. If you lose, you will not care.

Do not believe what they told you in grammar school. In the real world and in combat, violence solves *everything*.

To triumph in war, like in love, you must initiate contact.

It is usually easier to forgive an enemy *after* you have killed him.

Only imbeciles and fools fight fair (and will not do so for long).

Fools trust their enemies. Skepticism is the mother of survival.

The "Law of the Bayonet" says that the guy with the bullets wins.

Forget that "the harder they fall" foolishness. The bigger the bad guys are, the harder they punch, choke, and kick.

When a warrior buddies-up for combat, he should avoid pacifists and cowards (those who think with their legs).

Professional warriors should not trust the sniveling media whores. You have to "read between the lies."

Real warriors never get bogged down in a political war, where adversaries only shoot from the lip.

Hot garrison chow flown to the field is best. Hot field rations are better than cold field rations. Cold field rations are better than no food at all. Nonetheless, no food at all is still better than a cold rice ball a day, even though it may have little pieces of fish-head in it. *Never surrender!*

A warrior's pack, however heavy, is lighter than a POW's chains.

{Know warfare, know peace and safety;
{No knowledge of warfare, no peace and safety.

Even the Boy Scouts have figured it out: "Be Prepared."

Between firefights, *care packages* from home are great. Share everything, even the pound cake and cookies.

Without resupply, neither colonels nor corporals are combat ready.

In combat, air superiority is never a luxury.

Nonetheless, no one has yet discovered any type of *flying* that can prevent a Grunt from *walking*.

If you are convinced that you will lose, you are probably right.

In combat, last guys do not finish nice.

Day or night, incoming fire always has right-of-way.

Those who beat their swords into plowshares will plow for those who do not.

Artillery lends dignity to what otherwise would be a vulgar brawl.

Warriors engaged in combat in the tropics never wear underwear. Only they can appreciate why.

C-4 can make a dull day fun.

The raw intensity of a War Story is *inversely* proportional to the combat experience of the storyteller (a good way to identify wannabes and other non-combatants).

The number of mosquitoes at any given location is *inversely* proportional to your remaining amount of repellant.

The probability of diarrhea is *directly* proportional to the square of the thistle content of the local vegetation.

The urgency of the need to urinate is (1) *inversely* proportional to the temperature and (2) *directly* proportional to the layers of clothing you have to remove.

The combat effectiveness of any unit is *inversely* proportional to the amount of starch in its cammies.

The weight of your pack is *directly* proportional to the cube of the time you have been humping it.

The severity of the inclement weather is *directly* proportional to the amount of time you must be out in it.

When geared-up, the intensity of your itch is *inversely* proportional to the length of your reach.

The complexity of electronics equipment is *inversely* proportional to the IQ of the civilian instructors.

In a firefight, the seriousness of your wound is *directly* proportional to the distance to the nearest deep hole.

In a firefight, the difficulty of hearing a shouted order is *directly* proportional to the consequences for failing to carry it out.

In a firefight, the intensity of enemy fire is *directly* proportional to the curiousness of the enemy's target.

When you have run out of everything except the bad guys, you definitely are in combat.

If they are shooting at you, it is a high intensity conflict.

Always make sure somebody has a P-38 (for you new guys, a P-38 is a can opener -- and *more!*).

In war, winning is not always all it is cracked up to be -- the only genuine winner in the War of 1812 was Tchaikovsky (who would not be born for another 28 years).

In time of war, Hell hath no fury like a pacifist.

In combat, bad news may arrive in human waves.

Between firefights, letters from home are not always great. Both living and dying can hurt a lot.

If the sheltered REMFs are happy, the warriors in combat likely do not have what they need.

When it comes to War Stories, the farther the REMF storyteller was from the battle, the thicker the flak will be in his story.

In combat, discretion is the *bitter* part of valor.

Unfortunately, combat is not an efficient teacher. It gives the final test before presenting the lesson.

In combat a hero is no more brave than anyone else, but he is brave five minutes longer.

When you take a calculated risk in a life-and-death firefight, there usually are very few calculations.

Those who "live by the sword" will die when they attack those who fight with automatic weapons.

In combat the only perfect science is called hindsight.

"Subject Matter Experts" and "Professionals" have their place, but never get married to their ideas. Remember that (1) professionals built the *Titanic*, while (2) rank amateurs built the ark.

He who dies with the most toys is, nonetheless, dead.

After the battle, reputation is valuable, but honor is priceless.

Remember, if all of our warrior brothers do not come home, none of us can ever fully come home.

-- Murphy's Essential Dozen Rules for Firefights --

1. Never be the idiot who shows up armed only with a knife.

2. Bring an automatic weapon. Better yet, bring two.

3. Bring all of your friends, with all of *their* automatic weapons.

4. Bring **lots and lots** of ammo. It is cheap life insurance.

5. Make sure your weapons will fire *every time* (if angel-pee causes your weapons to jam, you will be terminally SOL).

6. If one of your weapons is a handgun, make sure its caliber begins with the numeral "4" or greater.

7. Have a good plan. Have a good back-up plan.

8. Any bad guy worth shooting is worth shooting several times.

9. Smoke and loud noise do not kill. Only hits count.

10. Remember that the "Hey-diddle-diddle" tactic works only in the movies. Be sneaky, always cheat, always win.

11. The faster you kill the bad guys, the less shot you will get.

12. Taking prisoners is (1) time consuming, (2) troublesome, and is (3) not recommended. Always kill **all** of the bad guys (if they are dead, they will make poor witnesses).

-- Murphy's Combat Tactics --

Do unto the enemy, and do it *first*.

If you do not strike first, you will be the first struck.

Speak softly, but *forget* the big stick. Carry a belt-fed weapon.

In combat, true happiness is always a belt-fed weapon.

In combat, always kill as many bad guys as you can. The ones you miss today may not miss you tomorrow.

If you can avoid it, never get into a fair fight.

If you can avoid it, never get into a fight without at least three times as much ammo as the other guy.

In combat, it is better for you to hump extra ammo than for your buddy to fill out your paperwork for Graves Registration.

Ammo is relatively cheap. Your life is not. In combat you can **never** hump too much ammo.

If you have extra ammo, even in a firefight, share quickly. You may be on the short end the next time around.

In a firefight, pace yourself. Otherwise, sooner or later you *will* run out of ammo -- usually at the worst possible time.

In general, the more ammo you have, the better. Nonetheless, it may spoil your day if, in a firefight, the type of ammo you have the most of is for the type of weapon you have the least of.

When given a choice, fight smarter, not harder.

Do what the enemy does not want you to do.

If at first your well-planned attack does not succeed, do not try again. Try something *different*.

If trying something different does not work, call in an airstrike.

In any firefight, nobody cares what you did yesterday, or what you may do tomorrow. The only thing that matters is what you are doing **right now**.

Cover your fellow warriors, so they will be around to cover you.

In combat, stay close. The farther you are from your warrior brothers, the less likely it is that they can help you when you need them the most.

When you have the enemy on the ground, kick him.

In combat, never look back unless you intend to go that way.

In a firefight, if you see two colonels conferring, you likely have fallen back a little too far.

If in command in a crisis, give all orders verbally. Never create a document that could wind up in a "Pearl Harbor" file.

If attacked by a fanatical, well armed, and numerically superior enemy force, it may be helpful to ponder: "How would the Lone Ranger handle this?"

On patrol and ambush, (1) never stand when you can sit, (2) never sit when you can lie down, (3) never stay awake when you can sleep, and (4) get in a good bowel movement whenever you can.

At night in combat, hang on to your gear. If you drop it during a fight, you can often find your canteen and E-tool right at your feet, but your ammo and grenades are probably lost forever.

Curious looking objects attract fire. Never lurk behind one.

When outnumbered in a firefight, shooting the bad guys is more important than radioing your plight to some REMF, miles away, who is incapable of assisting you.

In a firefight, he who hesitates is lost -- forever.

In a firefight, delay is the deadliest form of denial.

On the keyboard of combat, keep one finger on the escape key.

Always know when to "get out of Dodge."

In a firefight, (1) one problem is a problem, (2) two problems means it is time to get out of Dodge, but (3) three problems often means it is *too late* to get out of Dodge.

In combat, "what" generally is more important than "why" (when you see a snake, do not fret over why it is there, just kill it).

In combat, if something does not matter, it does not matter. The trick is to *make sure* that it does not matter.

A good plan today is always better than a great plan tomorrow.

On patrol and ambush, smart warriors always keep their eyes peeled, for he who sees first lives longest.

If you lose contact with the enemy, remember to look behind you.

Anything you do in combat can get you killed. Doing nothing will generally get you killed more quickly.

In a firefight, do *something*, even if it is wrong.

No matter how bad it gets, it is not over until it is over.

If you lose, and you are still alive, do not lose the reason.

-- Murphy's Combat Precautions --

Beware! Combat is always easier to get into than out of.

Once you are in the fight, it is too late to ponder whether or not it was a good idea.

Remember, you are not Superman, and you are not bulletproof.

Combat is not like Hollywood. In combat, getting shot *hurts*.

If you are in it, there is no such thing as a little firefight.

In combat, the best medal is the longevity medal.

In combat, prayer may not help, but it certainly can not hurt.

"Courage under fire" means that you are the only person who knows that you are afraid.

In a fight-to-the-death, a tie or a split decision is not a good option.

When you have run out of options in a firefight, if you think the enemy may be low on ammo, try to look unimportant.

Never try to draw fire. It irritates those around you.

In hi-tech, bio-weapon, and smart-weapon combat, there is no safety in numbers -- or in anything else.

Avoid all loud noises. There are few silent killers in combat.

Remember, the enemy may surrender, but his mines will not.

There are good plans, but there are no perfect plans. Beware, for your confidence may merely be your suspicion, asleep.

In combat, if everything is as clear as a bell, and things are going precisely as planned, look out! You are ripe for a surprise.

In combat a thorough mission briefing is a good idea, but do not get married to it. No plan has *ever* survived enemy contact, intact.

A warrior who thinks *small* bad guys can not be lethal in combat has never been in bed with a small rattlesnake.

When you have a clear choice in a crisis, opt for safety. That way, you will survive to be brave later on.

In combat, macho talk aside, *surviving* is more important than winning. You can only die once. But you can have many chances to win *if* you survive long enough to get them.

When your situation is desperate, it is too late to be serious.

He who hesitates under fire usually will not get another chance to.

When you are curled up deep in your hole, with mortars and artillery and bombs exploding all around, you can bet your bottom dollar that no atheists are lurking nearby.

If you suddenly find yourself in front of your unit in combat, they likely know something you do not.

In combat, rash decisions often bleed consequences.

Anyone can charge an enemy machinegun emplacement, across open terrain, alone, in broad daylight -- once.

When the pin has been pulled, Mr. Grenade is no longer our friend.

The bursting radius (killing range) of any grenade is *always* greater than your jumping range.

In combat it is inadvisable to buddy-up with someone whose grenade throwing range is less than the grenade killing range.

In a firefight, if you are keeping your head while all around you are losing theirs, perhaps you should reevaluate the situation.

A sucking chest wound is bad. But on the other hand, (1) all wounds are bad, and (2) all wounds suck.

Food for thought: your weapons were made by the lowest bidder.

A non-posthumous Purple Heart only proves you were (1) smart enough to think of a plan, (2) crazy enough to try it, and (3) lucky enough to survive.

Getting outnumbered and surrounded by the enemy is *always* a bad idea. (But on the bright side, it is a unique opportunity to get rid of the heavy ammo you have been humping.)

Before any firefight, it is bad luck to be superstitious.

Any bad guy with a rifle is a better shot than you with a pistol.

In a firefight, the greatest danger is the company of scared people.

But, a good scare is usually more effective than good advice.

If your attack is known in advance, it should not take place.

The concept of "survival of the fittest" is invalidated when some would-be hero insists on putting himself in a position where he will soon get himself killed.

After the fray, it is better to be a live lamb than a dead lion.

To appreciate the value of a single minute, ask any combat veteran what his friend was doing a minute before he got killed.

Helicopter resupply pilots will see you. Attack pilots on a close air support run will not. Dig your hole a little deeper.

-- Murphy's Combat Ironies --

No matter what you do, the bullet with your name on it will get you. So, also, can *random bullets* addressed "to whom it may concern" and *shrapnel* addressed to "occupant."

For each military action, there is an equal and opposite criticism.

When you have plenty of ammo, you never miss. When you are low on ammo, you can not hit squat.

The ammo you need *now* will be on the *next* chopper.

If you wear body armor, the enemy usually will miss that part.

In combat the only thing more accurate than incoming enemy fire is incoming friendly fire.

Most firefights occur at the junction of several maps. If you do not use paper maps, firefights occur when your batteries die.

Standard five-second fuses are so named because they burn in five seconds (plus or minus four).

If you can not remember, the Claymore is pointed toward you.

No combat-ready unit has ever passed inspection.

No inspection-ready unit has ever passed combat.

It is impossible to make any weapons system foolproof, because fools are deceptively ingenious.

In any wooded area at night, the sharp dead limbs on trees always will be at either (1) eye level or (2) groin level.

Professional enemy soldiers are predictable. Unfortunately, the world is full of dangerous amateurs.

Combat is not like Hollywood. In combat the cavalry does not always come to the rescue.

Combat, like love, is not called off on account of darkness.

If the enemy is within range, generally, so are you.

Radar fails (1) at night, or (2) in inclement weather, or (3) both.

Radios fail when you desperately need fire support.

If you make it hard for the enemy to get in, you can not get out.

The enemy always mines the *easy* way out.

The easy way usually will get you killed.

The enemy diversion you ignore usually is his main attack.

The enemy will attack when two conditions are met: (1) when he is ready, and (2) when you are not.

The enemy will attack *most ferociously* under two conditions: (1) on the darkest night, and (2) during a rainstorm.

The retreating enemy *squad* your platoon thinks it is pursuing is often an enemy *reconnaissance team*, luring you back to its entrenched *regiment* -- locked, loaded, and waiting.

Often, *military intelligence* is a contradiction in terms.

Fortify your front, and the enemy will attack your rear.

If your ambush is properly set, the enemy will never arrive.

If you are sufficiently dug in, the enemy will never attack.

The enemy has a penchant for turning your mines into equal opportunity weapons.

Superior firepower always prevails -- sometimes.

Combat experience is usually what we call our combat mistakes.

Warriors who take more than their fair share of objectives will get more than their fair share to take.

In combat, no order is so simple that it can not be misunderstood.

In a firefight, teamwork is essential. It gives the enemy someone else to shoot at.

The enemy never watches until you make a mistake.

If it worked in practice, it will fail in combat.

Things that must work together can not be shipped together.

-- Interchangeable parts *aren't*.

-- Friendly fire *isn't*.

-- Insect repellents *don't*.

-- Perfect plans *aren't* (and neither is the backup plan).

-- Recoilless rifles *aren't* (ask the idiot who stood behind one).

-- Waterproof clothing *isn't* (but it *does* retain perspiration).

-- Flash suppressors *do* (but only in the daytime).

-- Suppressive fires *won't* (except when they are directed onto abandoned positions).

-- Things that must be shipped together *aren't*.

-- Things that must work together *won't*.

Experience in combat is something you never have enough of until *after* you desperately need it.

The thing you need the most will be at the bottom of your pack.

If you need n crucial items from Supply, there will be $n-1$ in stock.

If your attack looks easy, it usually is hard. If your attack looks hard, it usually is impossible.

A slipping gear will allow your M-203 grenade launcher to fire when you least expect it. This may make you quite unpopular with what is left of your unit.

Unfortunately, tracers work both ways.

No matter which way you march, it is uphill and into the wind.

You will always be downwind when CS gas is used.

In combat, as in life, success occurs when you are alone. Failure occurs when everyone is watching.

Any stone in a boot migrates to the point of maximum pressure.

The weight of your pack can never remain uniformly distributed on the shoulder straps.

When hot garrison chow is flown to the field, it will rain.

In military intelligence, generally (1) the information you have is not what you want, (2) the information you want is not what you need, (3) the information you need is not available, and (4) everything depends on something else.

In combat, the side with the simplest uniform usually wins.

The crucial round will be a dud.

Military working dogs are trained to attack anything, including you.

About 15 percent of an intelligence report will be accurate and relevant. The trick is to figure out *which* 15 percent.

-- Murphy's Barracks Wisdom --

Unfortunately, no warrior fights all of the time. Between battles and wars, he and his military unit will retire in-the-rear-with-the-gear to rest and recuperate. There he will carouse, drink, brawl, and attempt to corrupt members of the opposite sex.

Warriors, your days in a barracks environment are fraught with potential peril. Here the *new enemy* smiles and shakes hands before stabbing you in the back. The soulless media whores, the mercenary purveyors of sensationalism and negativism, will leap at any opportunity to steal your honor. Worse yet, the parasitic liberal *politically correct* zealots will stop at nothing in attempts to drag you into the gutter of society with them. Therefore, all warriors in a barracks environment should remember:

Those who torture animals and wet the bed are either sex perverts or staff pogues. Both should be avoided.

When they can choose between a *politically correct* cry-baby and a true warrior, the media whores will interview the cry-baby.

Proven barracks admonitions for warriors:
  (a) Friends come and go, but enemies accumulate.
  (b) No decision, in your absence, will be in your best interests.
  (c) "You have the right to remain silent" is excellent advice.
  (d) The six time-tested responses calculated to avoid blame, in descending order of preference:
     (1) Who, me?
     (2) I wasn't there.
     (3) I didn't do it.
     (4) Nobody saw me do it.
     (5) You can't prove a thing.
     (6) That's my story, and I'm sticking to it.

Between wars, never delay (1) the end of a meeting, or (2) the start of Happy Hour.

Between wars, never let (1) a fool kiss you, or (2) a kiss fool you.

Between wars, (1) girlfriends are fair game, but (2) wives are not.

Murphy's Laws of Combat
for
Aviation

The history of military aviation is an immense sea of errors in which a few obscure truths may here and there be found. And like other occult techniques, aviation has a private jargon contrived to obscure its methods from non-practitioners.

Trying to fly without feathers was *never* easy. First came the hot air balloonists. They never killed anyone except themselves, from time to time. But on 17 December 1903 two brothers, Wilbur and Orville, started the aerial foolishness that still has us in trouble today. Because of those two culprits, aviation has gotten ever higher and faster, ever more complex and more dangerous.

Today flying machines of incredible lethality can swoop down into combat. Unfortunately, warriors have to *ride* or *fly* in these flimsy contraptions. For pilots and aircrewmen, the trick is to stay alive long enough to get the experience to enable them to stay alive a little longer. You Grunts just along for the ride, *think* about it. Maybe humping the hills on foot is not so bad after all.

In military aviation we find that the most deadly enemy is not the bad guys. The biggest threat comes from our own flying machines that *screw* (helicopters) or *suck and blow* (airplanes) their way through the sky. Therefore, to assist those who fly, Murphy offers his unique aeronautical knowledge in the following categories:

1. Murphy's Philosophy for Aviation
2. Murphy's Aviation Admonitions
3. Murphy's Aeronautical Ironies
4. Murphy's Infamous Military Aviation Predictions

-- Murphy's Philosophy for Aviation --

Gravity never loses. The best you can hope for is a draw.

Although fuel is a limited resource, gravity is forever.

In the ongoing battle between (1) military aircraft going hundreds of miles per hour, and (2) mountains going zero miles per hour, the mountains have yet to lose.

The three aviation constants: (1) airspeed is *life*, (2) altitude is *life insurance*, and (3) fuel is *more* life insurance.

The only time you have too much fuel is when you are on fire.

A combat aircrew lives in a world of perfection -- or not at all.

If all you can see out of the cockpit window is the ground, going round and round, and all you can hear is screaming in the cabin, something likely is amiss.

The mechanics of flying are simple. If you push the stick forward, the houses get bigger. If you pull the stick back, the houses get smaller. Of course, if you pull the stick back *too far*, the houses *very rapidly* get bigger again.

Assumption is the mother of most crashes.

Military flying consists of hours and hours of boredom, interrupted by brief moments of stark terror.

All take-offs are optional. But landing, *somewhere*, is mandatory.

You can land anywhere -- once.

When returning to Earth at high speed, the probability of survival is *inversely* proportional to the angle of arrival (large angle of arrival, small probability of survival, and vice versa).

While flying, you usually do not know what you do not know.

In combat, having a wingman is essential. He gives the enemy someone else to shoot at.

It is better to look bad than to die. But in military aviation it is easy to do both simultaneously.

There are (1) old combat aircrews, and there are (2) bold combat aircrews. But there are very few old **and** bold combat aircrews.

There is no such thing as a *routine* combat mission.

Superior pilots and aircrewmen use their superior judgement to avoid situations where they might have to use their superior skills.

If you do not know who the world's greatest pilot (or crew chief, or gunner, or loadmaster) is, it is not you.

While on your take-off roll, if an earthquake suddenly opens a 100 foot chasm across the runway and you crash into it, the mission of the Accident Board will be to find a way to blame it on pilot error.

Asking a military pilot what he thinks of the FAA is like asking a dog what he thinks about fire hydrants.

Any twin engine aircraft doubles your chance of engine failure. And after one engine has failed, the most common purpose of your other engine is to fly you to the scene of your accident.

Aerial combat is the perfect vocation for men who want to feel like boys, but not for men who still are.

There are aviation *rules*, and there are aviation *laws*. The rules were made by men, and can be suspended. The laws (of physics) were made by the Deity, and should not be trifled with.

A tactic, done twice without crashing, becomes a procedure.

Any pilot who relies on a "terminal forecast" can be sold the Brooklyn Bridge. Any pilot who relies on a "winds aloft" report can be sold Niagara Falls.

Flying at night is almost as easy as flying in the daytime, because the airplane does not know that it is dark.

You can get *anywhere* in ten minutes if you fly fast enough.

But, you have *never* been lost until you are lost at Mach 2.

The two worst things that can happen to an old aviator:
- (1) One day you will walk out to your aircraft, knowing that it will be your last flight.
- (2) One day you will walk out to your aircraft, *not* knowing that it will be your last flight.

-- Murphy's Aviation Admonitions --

When in doubt, climb! No one ever collided with the sky.

Remember, you can only *tie* the record for flying low.

If you absolutely must fly low, do not fly slow.

Pilots and aircrewmen who hoot with the owls by night should not try to soar with the eagles by day.

Never, never, never forget your priorities! No matter how bad it gets, *fly the aircraft!* Fly it until the last piece stops moving. Remember: (1) aviate, (2) navigate, (3) communicate.

Do not crash while trying to fly the radio. Aircraft fly because of the principle discovered by Bernoulli, not Marconi.

When a crash is inevitable, try to (1) strike the softest object in the vicinity, (2) as slowly and gently as possible.

When deviating from a rule, make your performance flawless (for example, if you fly under a bridge, try not to hit the bridge).

When flying VFR, stay out of the pretty little fluffy clouds, for mountains frequently lurk in them.

When the tanks are half empty, it is past time to review your plan.

Plan ahead. Keep checking. If you find yourself on the ground or sitting in your rubber raft -- looking up in the sky where your aircraft used to be -- it is too late to check your fuel gauge.

Never let your aircraft take you somewhere your brain did not get to five minutes earlier. Remember that you fly your aircraft with your *brain*, not with your hands.

In an aircraft in flight, if something is (1) red, (2) yellow, or (3) dusty, never touch it without a lot of forethought.

In combat, remember that your aircraft is not a tank. Your windshield is not hi-tech plastic that bullets bounce off of.

Aircraft weight/temperature/altitude charts are *tools*, not *rules*. Play it safe and make *two* trips (helicopter crews, take note).

Before take-off always pause and ponder: "How much does all that Grunt stuff in the cabin *really* weigh?"

The two most crucial absolutes in Aviation: (1) in airplanes, keep your airspeed up, and (2) in helicopters, keep your rotor RPM up; otherwise, the Earth will rise up and smite thee.

If you enjoy life, watch your six (fighter pilots, take note).

Never forget the six most useless things in Military Aviation:
1. The approach plates you did not bring.
2. The fuel you have burned.
3. The airspeed you had.
4. The altitude above you.
5. The runway behind you.
6. A tenth of a second ago.

When flying, pilots should try to stay in the middle of the air. The edges of the air can be recognized by the appearance of trees, buildings, telephone poles, the ground, the sea, and mountains. It is very difficult to fly beyond the edges of the air.

Fighter and Attack pilots: When your fear of the aircraft exceeds your fear of the ejection seat, it is time to say goodbye.

In an emergency when you have run out of bright ideas, luck may be a perfectly acceptable substitute. But in the long run, trusting luck alone is not conducive to longevity.

In aviation you start with (1) a bag full of luck and (2) an empty bag of experience. The trick is to fill your bag of experience before you empty your bag of luck.

Airspeed, Altitude, Brains. You need at least *two* at all times.

-- Murphy's Aeronautical Ironies --

Combat *flying* is not dangerous. Crashing is what is dangerous.

Combat flying is not like a video game. When flying, you can not push a button and start over.

When flying in combat, being *good* and being *lucky* sometimes is still not good enough.

A thunderstorm usually is not quite as bad on the inside as it looks on the outside. It is worse.

In military aviation, everything that goes up must come down. Going up is usually easy. It is the manner of *coming down* that can spoil your whole day.

In a crisis it is always better to break ground and head into the wind, than to break wind and head into the ground.

In a crisis it is always better to be on the ground, wishing you were flying, than to be flying, wishing you were on the ground.

The farther you fly over the mountains at night, the stronger the strange fuselage vibrations will become.

Day or night, the most crucial radio frequencies will be illegible.

Combat flight experience is something you never have enough of until *after* you desperately need it.

In retractable gear aircraft, if it takes over 80% power to taxi, you probably have landed gear-up.

There are three simple rules for making smooth landings, but no one knows what they are.

A smooth landing is mostly luck, two in a row is all luck, and three in a row is lying.

When flying, you are never lost if you do not care where you are.

In combat it is true that more aircraft are downed by a shortage of spare parts than by enemy fire. The big difference is that few pilots and aircrewmen *die* because of a shortage of spare parts.

A competent pilot has mastered a host of complex skills. A competent aircrewman can perform myriad functions. Yet, none of these skills and functions guarantee survival in combat.

-- Murphy's Infamous Military Aviation Predictions --

Heavier-than-air flying machines are impossible.
  [Lord Kelvin, President of the Royal Society, 1895]

It is complete and utter nonsense to believe that flying machines will ever work.
  [Sir Stanley Mosley, philosopher, 1905]

We soon saw that the helicopter had no future, so we dropped it. The helicopter does, with great labor, only what the balloon does without labor. The helicopter is no more fitted than the balloon for rapid horizontal flight. If its engine stops, it must fall with deathly violence, for it can neither glide like an aeroplane nor float like a balloon. The helicopter is easier to design than the aeroplane. But, it is utterly worthless!

[Wilbur Wright, co-developer and pilot of the world's first successful airplane in 1903, writing in 1909]

We do not consider that aeroplanes will be of any possible use for war purposes.

[Report of the British Secretary of State for War, 1910]

Airplanes are interesting toys, but are of no military value.

[Marshall Ferdinand Foch, Professor of Strategy, 1911]

The aeroplane is an invention of the devil. It will never play any part in the defense of the nation, my boy!

[Sir Sam Hughes, Canadian Minister of Defence, 1914]

"Aaaaahhh, sh--[an expletive]."

[According to McDermott Associates (specialists in cockpit voice recorders), the most common *final words* on cockpit voice recorder tapes of airliners which have crashed. Usually voiced with resignation -- no emotion, no panic, no sarcasm. Basically an acknowledgement that all that could be done, had been done.]

Murphy's Special Laws
for
Helicopters

All of "Murphy's Laws of Combat for Aviation" which apply to fixed-wing aircraft also apply to helicopters.

But helicopters are *different*. They kill you *quickly*. No matter how good you are, no matter how lucky you are, no matter how much your mother loves you, a helicopter can kill you in the twinkling of an eye. The impending peril for helicopter crews and passengers was summed up by Harry Reasoner on *ABC Evening News* on 16 February 1971, when he stated:

A helicopter does not want to fly. It is maintained in the air by a variety of forces and controls working in opposition to each other. And if there is any disturbance in this delicate balance, the helicopter stops flying immediately and disastrously.

There is no such thing as a gliding helicopter. That is why being a helicopter pilot is so different from being an airplane pilot. Airplane pilots are open clear-eyed buoyant extroverts, and helicopter pilots are brooding introspective anticipators of trouble. They know that if something bad has not happened, it is about to.

A helicopter can kill you more quickly than any other instrument ever conceived by the mind of man. And in combat, helicopters habitually fly to evil places where the enemy can kill you quickly, too. Therefore, pilots, crew chiefs, gunners, and loadmasters must *always remember* five things about flying helicopters:

1. In a helicopter, eternal vigilance is the price of survival.
2. There is no such thing as a gliding helicopter.
3. The safest helicopter is the one that can barely kill you.
4. You are always a student in a helicopter.
5. If at first you do not succeed, ***never*** try autorotations again.

To give helicopter pilots and aircrewmen a glimmer of hope of surviving, Murphy offers invaluable insight about their fling-wing machines. Anyone foolish enough to consider flying, or riding, in a helicopter should carefully study the following sub-chapters:

1. Murphy's Unique Philosophy for Helicopters
2. Murphy's Admonitions for Helicopter Crews
3. Murphy's Rules for Learning to Fly Helicopters

-- Murphy's Unique Philosophy for Helicopters --

Any mechanical contraption that attempts to screw its way into the sky is doomed to failure.

According to laws of physics and aerodynamics, helicopters can not fly. They are just so ugly that the Earth repels them.

In helicopters the foreseeable future is the next five seconds. Long range planning is the next two minutes.

Helicopters are tricky machines. Helicopter crews measure their lives in days, not years.

When your helicopter "wings" are leading and lagging, precessing and flapping, sinister forces are at play.

The aerodynamic phenomena known as (1) Vortex Ring State, (2) Retreating Blade Stall, and (3) Power Settling are nothing more than fancy ways to describe instant death.

Helicopter crews fly with an intensity akin to "spring loaded" while waiting for pieces of their craft to fly off.

You can always identify a helicopter crewman in a car, boat, or train. He (1) never smiles, he (2) listens to the machine, and he (3) always hears something he thinks is not quite right.

At any small airport there are lots of old airplanes lying around, but you *never* see an old helicopter -- *think* about it.

The terms *protective armor* and *helicopter* are mutually exclusive.

Whoever said "the pen is mightier than the sword" never flew in a helicopter in a AAA and missile threat environment.

Repeatedly flying helicopters into a AAA and missile threat environment does not require only courage. It requires stupidity.

When (1) the weather is clear, (2) the rotors are in track, (3) the fuel tanks are full, and (4) all gauges are in the green, you are about to be surprised. That is just what helicopters do.

There are two types of combat aircraft, (1) fighters and (2) targets. Unfortunately a helicopter is not a fighter.

In fixed-wing aircraft, (1) airspeed is *life* and (2) altitude is *life insurance*. But in helicopters, rotor RPM is *everything!*

Sudden loud noises in the helicopter *will* get your undivided attention. This is especially true (1) at night, (2) while IFR, and (3) while over the mountains or ocean.

The three best things in life are (1) a good orgasm, (2) a good landing, and (3) a much needed bowel movement. For a helicopter crew, a successful return from an emergency night medevac is a unique opportunity to experience them all at the same time.

In combat there is no such thing as a *secure* LZ. Anyone who says otherwise is selling something.

On any medevac, the amount of time you must spend in the LZ is *directly* proportional to the intensity of enemy fire.

On emergency night medevacs, the LZ coordinates usually will be at the junction of several maps.

Among helicopter crews after a successful emergency ammo resupply at night, the *first* liar does not stand a chance.

Flying is better than riding in a vehicle, which is better than running, which is better than walking, which is better than crawling -- all of which are better than an *emergency night medevac* under fire in a helicopter, although it is *technically* a form of flying.

Will Rogers never met a fighter pilot.

Fighter pilots make movies, but helicopter crews make history.

-- Murphy's Admonitions for Helicopter Crews --

For a military pilot or aircrewman, helicopter time in your logbook is akin to S.T.D. in your Health Record.

Flying in a helicopter is about the same as masturbating. It *may* be fun at the time, but it is nothing to brag about in public.

Rotor RPM *must* be kept within the green arc. Failure to heed this admonition will adversely affect the morale of the crew.

When flying helicopters, the main trick is to keep the fuselage from turning as fast as the rotors.

If everything is working properly on your helicopter, consider yourself temporarily lucky.

When flying a military helicopter, keep checking. There is always something you have missed.

Simultaneously running out of (1) airspeed, (2) altitude, (3) rotor RPM, (4) luck, and (5) bright ideas will ruin your day.

Running out of (1) collective, (2) pedal, (3) forward cyclic, or (4) aft cyclic are all exceptionally bad ideas.

If your engine fails you have 3/10 of a second to either (1) lower the collective, or (2) begin flying like a manhole cover.

In combat, helicopter crews usually fly on a reactive basis. So, (1) eat when you can, (2) sleep when you can, and (3) defecate when you can. Your next opportunity may not come around for a long, long time.

Flying a helicopter at an altitude in excess of 250 feet is considered risky and downright foolish.

If you ditch at sea in a helicopter, get out immediately. It will sink in 20 seconds (plus or minus about 19).

In combat it is, generally speaking, unwise to make an emergency helicopter landing in any enemy-infested area that our fixed-wing friends have recently bombed or strafed.

In a military helicopter, *death* is the price you pay for trying to look Sierra Hotel.

Non-practitioners: ***never, never*** walk up behind an old helicopter crewman and clap your hands (*trust Murphy* on this one).

-- Murphy's Rules for Learning to Fly Helicopters --

A few final words for you warriors who are non-practitioners in the helicopter world. You may be an airplane pilot or crewman with an urge to expand your skills. Or you may be a Grunt, a professional population control specialist, with a dream of learning to fly helicopters.

No problem. If you can drive a car, why not try helicopters? Just follow Murphy's six simple easy-to-understand steps:

Step 1: *Think* about it. Physicists, aerodynamic experts, and scientists have no idea what holds a helicopter up. But whatever it is, it could stop at any moment. Go to Step 2.

Step 2: After pondering the issue, in all probability you should forget the whole thing. If not, go to Step 3.

Step 3: In the helicopter, sit by someone who actually knows how to fly the thing. Let *him* fly it. Go to Step 4.

Step 4: In flight, when told to take the controls, **refuse**! (Hint: this is very important.) Do not *touch* anything. If you should *inadvertently* touch something, *do not move it.* Your options are: (A) Return to Step 2. (B) If your life insurance premiums are current, you may go to Step 5.

Step 5: Never, ***never*** let the pilot (the guy who knows how to fly the thing) demonstrate an *autorotation.* That is when you cut the engine off and drop like a pallet of bricks. It is sort of like *bungee jumping*, except that it is (A) straight down, (B) at warp speed, (C) with no bungee, and (D) you know you are going to die. Yet, if by virtue of some miracle you *survive* the impact, go to Step 6.

Step 6: Return to Step 2.

Landing In Trees: A power-off landing into a heavily wooded area should be accomplished by executing a normal autorotative approach and flare. The flare should be executed so as to reach zero rate-of-descent and zero ground speed as close to the tops of the trees as possible . . . .
   [***believe it or not***, a verbatim excerpt from Section 5-36, NATOPS Manual, CH-46D Helicopter]

Murphy's Military Superlatives

The best, the worst. The smartest, the dumbest. Listed here are Murphy's Military Superlatives, gleaned from archives throughout the world. Wise warriors will learn from these abstracts, which reflect both the *high's* and the *low's* of military art and culture:

-- World's Best Draft Notice --

Everyone will now be mobilized and all boys old enough to carry a spear will be sent to Addis Ababa. Married men will take their wives to carry food and cook. Those without wives will take any woman without a husband. Women with small babies need not go. The blind, those who cannot walk, or those who for any reason cannot carry a spear, are exempted. Anyone found at home after the receipt of this order will be hung.
[Ethiopian Draft Notice, 1935]

-- World's Best Literary Tribute to Warriors --

Cowards die many times before their deaths;
The valiant never taste of death but once.
[William Shakespeare (1564-1616); *Julius Caesar*]

-- World's Most "Famous Last Words" from a Warrior --

Hurry! Hurry! We've caught them napping!
[MGen. George A. Custer, USA, commander of the Seventh Cavalry, U.S. Army; to the messenger (*the sole survivor*) he was dispatching to ride to Capt. Frederick Benteen with a request for more ammunition, after discovering an Indian village that he planned to attack immediately (**Bad Decision**: the village near the Little Big Horn River contained roughly 6500 warriors from the eleven tribes of the Confederated Sioux Nation; these warriors

outnumbered Custer's troopers 24-to-1; they chased the 266 troopers to a nearby ridge and killed them all), 25 June 1876]

-- World's Best Philosophy for Warriors --

Do not fear the enemy, for, at the worst, he can only take your life. Instead, a wise warrior fears *the media*, for he knows the sniveling media whores may steal his honor.
[SSgt. Robert Johnson, USA; responding to a question from a high school student who had asked about a soldier's greatest fear in combat, in Fort Worth, Texas, August 2001]

-- World's Worst Military Prediction --

A million Marines can not take Tarawa in a hundred years.
[RAdm. Keiji Shibasaki, Imperial Japanese Navy, Commander of the Japanese garrison on Tarawa; the month before 5600 U.S. Marines assaulted the island fortress on 20 November 1943 and conquered it in 76 bloody hours]

-- World's Best Solution for Cowardice --

We don't want yellow cowards in this Army. They should be killed off like rats! If not, they will go home after the war is over and breed more cowards . . . Kill off the [expletive] cowards and we will have a nation of brave men.
[Gen. George S. Patton Jr., USA; in an address to the soldiers of his Third Army, in England, 5 June 1944]

-- World's Best Military Credo --

The U.S. Navy steams *Full Speed Ahead*, and the U.S. Air Force likes to *Aim High*. The U.S. Army tells each soldier to *Be All You Can Be*. The famed daredevil French Zouaves chanted their *Huzzah*, and victorious Japanese warriors shouted *Banzai*. The international fighter pilot's bar-room cheer invoked gallows humor, *Hurrah for the next man to die!* In Texas the warriors of the volunteer militia vowed to *Remember the Alamo!* Worldwide there are many other military credos. Here is Murphy's choice for the absolute, hands down, world's best:

Death Before Dishonor!
   [the credo of a U.S. Marine -- for trivia devotees, it is also the most popular *tattoo* among U.S. Marines]

-- Fighting Words from American Warriors --

In the heat of battle, or in preparation for battle, Fighting Words epitomize the courageous aggressive ethos of the professional American Warrior. Fighting Words demonstrate the will to win at all costs. Murphy has picked four statements which exemplify the tenacious warrior spirit necessary for success in battle:

United States Army: To the German Commander:
                                   NUTS!
                         The American Commander
   [BGen. Anthony C. McAuliffe, USA; acting commander of the surrounded and beleaguered 101st Airborne Division at Bastogne, Belgium, in a typewritten reply to the German Army ultimatum that he surrender or be annihilated, 22 December 1944]

United States Navy: Damn the torpedoes, full speed ahead!
   [Adm. David G. Farragut, USN; aboard his *USS Hartford* entering Mobile Bay, Alabama, after Confederate Navy mines sunk the leading warships in his armada, 5 August 1864]

United States Marine Corps: Come on, you sons of bitches! Do you want to live forever?
   [GySgt. Daniel J. "Dan" Daly, USMC; as he led his men in the bayonet charge that routed entrenched German Army defenders in Belleau Wood near Lucy 'le Bocage, France, 6 June 1918]

United States Air Force: We're going to bomb them back into the Stone Age.
   [Gen. Curtis E. LeMay, USAF; in a statement to the Joint Chiefs of Staff outlining his plan to deal with the growing crisis in Indochina (the Joint Chiefs vetoed his plan), May 1964]

-- Motivational Shouts for American Warriors --

The medieval Gallic hordes of western Europe had their chilling *battle cry*. The indigenous American Indians had their *war whoop*. The grey-clad Confederate Army infantry had its famed *rebel yell*. In combat these shouts were intended to (1) motivate fellow warriors and (2) strike terror within the ranks of the enemy.

Today in a barracks environment all gung-ho American Warriors use Motivational Shouts. Warriors use these verbal exclamations to display enthusiasm and agreement, loyalty and dedication:

U.S. Army: Hoo-ah!
U.S. Navy: Full Speed Ahead!
U.S. Marine Corps: Ooo-rah!
U.S. Air Force: Air Power!

-- Military Academies for American Warriors --

Throughout the ages, history has proved that successful warrior leaders have been properly schooled in military art and science. Therefore, America maintains three collegiate-level academies to prepare her premier warrior candidates for leadership in combat:

U.S. Army: United States Military Academy, West Point, New York.
U.S. Navy: United States Naval Academy, Annapolis, Maryland.
U.S. Marine Corps: United States Naval Academy (see above).
U.S. Air Force: United States Air Force Academy, Colorado Springs, Colorado.

-- Combat Philosophy of American Warriors --

American Warriors share a simple combat philosophy: they intend to win by *killing the enemy*. Over the years, America's elite warriors have voiced their battle plans in a host of ways, including the belly-ripping statements Murphy has selected, below:

United States Army: Nobody ever won a war by dying for his country. You win a war by making the *other* poor dumb bastard die for *his* country.
[Gen. George S. Patton Jr., USA; addressing the soldiers of his Third Army, in England, 5 June 1944]

United States Navy: Praise the Lord and pass the ammunition!
[Lt. Howell M. Forgy, USN Chaplain; to the Navy antiaircraft gun crews aboard the *USS New Orleans* during the Japanese air attack at Pearl Harbor, Hawaii, 7 December 1941]

United States Marine Corps: Those poor bastards. They've got us surrounded. Good! Now we can fire in any direction. They won't get away this time!
[Col. Lewis B. "Chesty" Puller, USMC; speaking to his staff after his Intelligence Officer discovered that the First Marine Regiment was surrounded and outnumbered 18-to-1 by seven Chinese Divisions at Chosin Reservoir, Korea, December 1950]

United States Air Force: I can break up Russia's five A-bomb nests in a week. And when I go up to meet Christ, I think I could explain to Him that I had saved civilization.
[MGen. Orvil A. Anderson, USAF; explaining his plan to prevent the Soviet Union from entering the Korean War to aid North Korea (civilian authorities vetoed the plan), winter 1950]

-- Most Decorated American Warriors --

Nitpickers searching for a subjective selection of honorees have hit the jackpot. Military *decorations* (for the uninformed, that means *medals*) can not be mathematically quantified.

No one can equitably compare a Bronze Star to a Distinguished Flying Cross, or a Purple Heart to the Legion of Merit. Like apples and oranges, they are not the same thing. Also, no one can substantiate that a Medal of Honor (the nation's highest award for valor) carries more weight than three Silver Star awards.

To further muddy the water, military medals are awarded under three circumstances: (1) for personal valor in combat, (2) for leadership or excellence, and (3) to entire military units that have excelled.   There is a world of difference between an award for personal valor in combat, and an award to a person whose only claim to fame is that he was a *member* of a decorated unit.

In making selections, Murphy used simple criteria. The selectee must have received the majority of his awards for personal valor in combat (REMFs, in-the-rear-with-the-gear leaders, administrative pogues, bean counters, chaplain's assistants, and mail clerks were not considered). Further, the selectee must have been awarded at least one Purple Heart, and he must have "loved to fight."

In addition to enemy bullet holes in his body, Murphy noted that each of the selectees shared another trait in common. Each of them originally *enlisted* in the military.   In fact, the Navy selectee remained an enlisted warrior throughout his career. The Air Force selectee, who retired as a colonel, began his military career as an enlisted Marine who spent three years fighting and bleeding his way across the South Pacific in combat in World War II:

U.S. Army: Maj. Audie L. Murphy (1924-1971)
U.S. Navy: BMC James E. Williams (1930-1999)
U.S. Marine Corps: LtGen. Lewis B. "Chesty" Puller (1898-1971)
U.S. Air Force: Col. George E. "Bud" Day (1925--)

-- Best Beer-Drinking Song for American Warriors --

Wine, wild women, and *song* are synonymous with the fighting culture of American Warriors. They can not be separated. A night of alcoholic revelry the evening before battle serves to boost the spirits, promote camaraderie, and ensure restful sleep.

The best beer-drinking song for American Warriors? Once again, Murphy will have to make a subjective choice. Without question, the unanimous choice *should* be the raunchy warrior's rendition of *Let Me Call You Sweetheart*. Too bad, because only the first line can be printed. The rest of the song is beyond offensive, beyond profane, beyond obscene; it establishes a brave new frontier for vulgarity -- the absolute greatest beer-drinking song! But it would burn a hole through any paper it was printed on.

Therefore, Murphy has decided to compromise. Murphy has picked two beer-drinking songs, one for ground-pounders and another for aerial warriors: Murphy has listed the primary stanza, followed by the musical bridge (for ignorami, *musical bridge* means a (1) refrain with a (2) change of tempo and tune):

-- for ground-pounding warriors --
In peacetime we Regulars are happy,
In peacetime we're willing to serve;
But just when we get a war started,
We'll call out the [expletive] Reserves.
　　Call out! Call out!
　　Call out the [expletive] Reserves, Reserves!
　　Call out! Call out!
　　Call out the [expletive] Reserves!

-- for aerial warriors --
Gory, gory, what a hell of a way to die!
Gory, gory, what a hell of a way to die!
Stall! Spin! Crash, burn, and die!
And he'll never fly home again!
　　Ten-thousand [expletive] dollars going home to his wife,
　　Ten-thousand [expletive] dollars in exchange for his life;
　　More [expletive] money than she's seen in her life,
　　Think of all the goodies she can buy!

-- Birthdays for American Warriors --

Murphy has some *revisionist* history to offer. The United States of America did not exist on paper until 4 July 1776. After that, five years of combat were needed to ensure the survival of the new nation. But in mid-1775 before the United States was born, the *Continental Congress* had established the *Continental* Army, the *Continental* Navy, and the *Continental* Marines.

It was not until later that the *United States Congress* created the *United States* Army, Navy, and Marine Corps. Nonetheless, today these three branches of the U.S. Armed Forces recognize the dates listed below (when their *continental* forebears were established) as their official birthday.

During the first half of the 1900s the U.S. Army began using aircraft in combat. These aircraft, the aircrews, and the support personnel formed the *U.S. Army Air Corps*, also called the U.S.

Army Air Service and the U.S. Army Air Forces. In 1947 the U.S. Congress officially established the U.S. Air Force:

U.S. Army: 14 June 1775
U.S. Navy: 13 October 1775
U.S. Marine Corps: 10 November 1775
U.S. Air Force: 18 September 1947

-- Motion Pictures for American Warriors --

Another subjective list! Some hand-wringing critics may debate these choices that Murphy has made.

Many people would select *The Green Berets* as the premier Army film. These advocates could point out that it (1) starred America's foremost screen warrior, John Wayne, (2) that it was the number one box office draw of its day, and (3) that the patriotic theme song was simultaneously number one on the Hit Parade. But if you want the *politically impossible* "Old Blood and Guts" and his gung-ho philosophy on offensive warfare, you pick *Patton*.

Also, many may question Murphy's selection of *The D.I.* as the best Marine Corps film. Fans of John Wayne probably think that his immortal *Sands of Iwo Jima* should have gotten the nod. Yet, after watching Jack Webb put his recruits through Marine Corps boot camp, *The D.I.* remains Murphy's top choice.

For the best Navy movie, warrior wannabes probably pick either *Top Gun* or *An Officer and a Gentleman*. Both films are OK if what you truly want is romantic fantasy. But those looking for a slice of history, butt-kicking naval battles (with lots of original, but colorized, WW II combat footage), and the victorious American underdog will agree with Murphy's first choice, *Midway*.

For the best Air Force film, some may favor *Twelve O'Clock High* and the solemn philosophy of Gen. Frank Savage: "Consider yourselves already dead; once you accept that idea, it won't be so tough." But for a chilling "you-are-there" ride over Nazi Germany in a shot-to-splinters B-17, fortified with reels of colorized WW II aerial combat film, Murphy picks the best, *Memphis Belle*.

In addition to the name of the selected motion picture, Murphy also has included (1) the year the film debuted and (2) the name of the primary starring actor:

U.S. Army:	*Patton*, 1970; George C. Scott
U.S. Navy:	*Midway*, 1976; Charlton Heston
U.S. Marine Corps:	*The D.I.*, 1957; Jack Webb
U.S. Air Force:	*Memphis Belle*, 1990; Matthew Modine

-- Best Nicknames for American Warriors --

Murphy knows dozens of nicknames for America's warriors. Unfortunately, most of the Army nicknames are unprintable, and Navy nicknames run the gauntlet from "swabbie" to "paint-picker" to other descriptive names that wannabes would not understand. So, according to Murphy, here are the most appropriate monikers:

U.S. Army:	Doggie
U.S. Navy:	Squid
U.S. Marine Corps:	Jarhead
U.S. Air Force:	Zoomie

-- Military Colors for American Warriors --

The U.S. Army, Navy, Marine Corps, and Air Force each have two official colors, which Murphy has listed below:

U.S. Army:	Black and Gold
U.S. Navy:	Blue and Gold
U.S. Marine Corps:	Gold and Scarlet
U.S. Air Force:	Ultramarine Blue and Golden Yellow

-- Military Anthems for American Warriors --

The first Army anthem was *The Caisson Song*. The first Navy anthem had the same title and tune it retains today, but all of the stanzas had different words -- about a football game.

Below is the name of the current anthem for each of the armed forces. For a history of each anthem (and its predecessor, where applicable), plus the words of all stanzas, see the chapter, "Anthems of the Armed Forces and the National Anthem."

U.S. Army: *The Army Goes Rolling Along*
U.S. Navy: *Anchors Aweigh*
U.S. Marine Corps: *The Marines' Hymn*
U.S. Air Force: *Off We Go into the Wild Blue Yonder*

-- Mottos of American Warriors --

U.S. Army: This We'll Defend (the flag)
U.S. Navy: Not Self, but Country (unofficial)
U.S. Marine Corps: Semper Fidelis (meaning, *Always Faithful)*
U.S. Air Force: Peace Is Our Profession (unofficial)

-- Unofficial Mascots of American Warriors --

Murphy has listed the *unofficial* mascots for the U.S. Armed Forces. The mule, goat, and falcon are the *official* mascots of the U.S. Military Academy, the U.S. Naval Academy, and the U.S. Air Force Academy, respectively. The English Bulldog mascot of the Marine Corps stems from the *teufel-hunden* (meaning, *devil-dogs*) name given to the Marines by the German Army in World War I. Shortly thereafter, Marine recruiting posters featured a caricature of a U.S. Marine bulldog chasing a terrified German poodle.

U.S. Army: Mule
U.S. Navy: Goat
U.S. Marine Corps: English Bulldog
U.S. Air Force: Falcon

-- Best Invention for the American Warrior --

P-38: Today, American Warriors dine on MREs: Meals, Ready to Eat. But in World War II and for years thereafter, warriors got their cuisine in cans and paper packages known as C-Rations. They needed a compact can-opener to open the cans, so in 1942 the Subsistence Research Laboratory developed the P-38.

Only an inch and a half long, the aluminum P-38 is a simple, lightweight, folding-blade, multipurpose tool. It not only opens cans, but it serves as a knife, screwdriver, or whatever. A small hole allows warriors to thread the P-38 onto their dog tag chain.

No one is sure how the P-38 got its name. Some maintain that it stemmed from the 38 punctures required to circumnavigate the top of a C-Ration can. Others say the moniker is based on the popular claim that the nifty new tool worked with the speed of the then-state-of-the-art P-38 fighter plane.

Regardless of the origin of the name, the P-38 still lives on today, decades after C-Rations were relegated to the history books. The fame of the P-38 stems from the unique blend of ingenuity and creativity of the warriors who still use it. Today it is almost impossible to find a crusty old warrior of yesteryear who does not still have his trusty and treasured old P-38.

-- Most Politically In-Correct Statement for American Warriors --

The feminization of the military has been, and remains, a cancer eating away at the warrior spirit and preparedness of the U.S. military.

[Geoff Metcalf, in "Run Jane, Run," 16 July 2001]

-- Best Epitaph for an American Warrior --

In 480 BC the Spartan Warriors who sacrificed all while holding the pass at Thermopylae earned their epitaph; they each remained eternally "obedient to the laws."

Over 2000 years later in the United States, the tombstones of many American Warriors relate the circumstances of their deaths in battle. For some the epitaph is brief. For PFC Thomas Willis, USA, it reads: "Killed In Action on Normandy Beachhead."

Other epitaphs offer detail. The tombstone of LtCol. Clarence K. Hollingsworth, USA, notes: "He died May 16, 1945, in Belgium, of wounds received in action on April 14, 1945, in Germany."

Some epitaphs contain eloquent inspirational wording. 1stLt. William M. Rogers, CSA, was killed-in-action on 18 October 1863, and his tombstone notes: "In defence of Southern Rights he laid upon his Country's Altar a life full of the highest promise, in the triumphs of Faith and in hope of a brighter world."

Murphy made a subjective choice. His selection for the best epitaph for an American Warrior follows:

> And when he gets to Heaven,
> To St. Peter, he will tell:
> "Another Marine reporting, sir;
> I've served my time in Hell."

[tombstone epitaph of PFC William Cameron, USMC (H Co., 2nd Bn., First Marines); killed-in-action near Lunga Point on Guadalcanal, Solomon Islands, in the South Pacific, 1942]

-- Most Patriotic Statement by an American Warrior --

We are *honored* to have had the *opportunity* to serve our Country under difficult circumstances. We are profoundly *grateful* to our Commander-and-Chief and to our Nation for this day. God bless America!

[Capt. Jeremiah A. Denton, USN; an A-6 attack pilot who had been shot down on 18 July 1965 and imprisoned as a POW in North Vietnam for almost eight years. Denton was the senior officer among the first group of POWs to be released. When the C-141 rolled to a stop at Clark AFB in the Philippines, Denton was the first man to exit the aircraft. With dozens of TV cameras rolling, he walked to a waiting microphone and spoke these three short sentences, 13 February 1973]

-- Best American Warrior Philosophy on Terrorists --

They should be caught, drawn & quartered, decapitated, and their ugly [expletive] heads put on pikes in front of the White House.

[Maj. Bill F. Weaver, USMC; 12 September 2001]

-- American Warriors' Reflections on Combat --

Warriors who have tasted combat know that warfare is not glamour and glory. Warfare, although often necessary in the course of world affairs, is obscene beyond mortal description. Murphy suggests that young boys and warrior wannabes should soberly reflect upon these statements by American Warriors:

U.S. Army: There is many a boy here today who looks on war as all glory. But, boys, war is Hell!
[Gen. William T. Sherman, USA; addressing a patriotic gathering of military veterans and young men, 12 August 1880]

U.S. Navy: Don't cheer, men. The poor devils are dying.
[Capt. John W. Philip, USN; to the crew of his *USS Texas* as they steamed past the burning Spanish warship *Vizcaya* at Santiago, Cuba, 3 July 1898]

U.S. Marine Corps: How can I feel like a hero, when I hit the beach with two-hundred-and-fifty buddies, and only twenty-seven of us walked off alive?
[PFC Ira A. Hayes, USMC; speaking on 16 April 1945 in reply to a remark about his role in raising the American flag atop Mt. Suribachi, Iwo Jima, on 23 February 1945]

U.S. Air Force: He was burning to death in the plane and couldn't get out. He was [screaming for] someone to tell his wife that he loved her, and for someone to shoot him.
[Chaplain Ray Stubbe, USN; *The Final Formation*, 1995, quoting a witness to the death of a U.S. Air Force pilot at Khe Sanh, Vietnam, on 23 August 1967]

Tragically, what mankind has learned from centuries of warfare is that mankind has not learned much from centuries of warfare.

Murphy's Guide
for
Warriors Who Drink Beer

Beer and warfare have gone hand-in-hand since time immemorial. The fabled Roman Legions of Julius Caesar were appropriately wined and dined the night before battle. Wine (supplemented with wild wanton women and song) fired the spirit, deadened the senses, and led to a restful sleep. Without their wine, women, and song, Roman centurions would have had to soberly contemplate the next day's perils and hardships -- not a good idea.

In recent years, modern medical science has established a proven biological truism: the consumption of beer kills brain cells. In so doing, beer consumption enhances human health and vitality.

To fully understand this phenomenon, one should consider the attrition characteristics of a herd of antelopes. The herd will never abandon its old, weak, or diseased members. Therefore, the herd moves only as fast as the slowest and weakest antelope can travel. When the herd is hunted by predators, it tries to run away. But because the herd must not outrun the weakest antelopes, the slow animals in the rear of the herd are killed first.

This natural attrition is beneficial. Killing only the weak or diseased antelopes improves the general health of the herd. This culling process validates the concept of "survival of the fittest."

In the same manner, the human brain can function only as fast as its slowest brain cells. When we drink beer, alcohol naturally attacks and kills these slowest and weakest brain cells first. With these weak brain cells eliminated, the human brain can function more rapidly. The more beer we drink, the more weak brain cells we kill. Consequently, the more beer we consume, the more we enhance the overall health and efficiency of our brain.

Beer, the modern health and nutrition supplement! Think about it; there are 24 hours in a day, and 24 beers in a case. It can not possibly be a mere coincidence! Also, nutritionists have proven that the perfect "balanced diet" is a beer in each hand.

After a wise warrior reads about all of the evils of drinking, he usually gives up reading. He finds that if he stays wasted most of the time, his time is never truly wasted. And if a woman drives him to drink, he always has the decency to thank her. Plus, he learns a valuable lesson. If he always does, *sober*, what he said he would do, *drunk*, it teaches him to keep his mouth shut.

Yet, a wise warrior should drink responsibly. He knows that excessive consumption of beer may lead to otherwise inexplicable rug burns on his forehead. Too much beer can convince him that he can converse with others without spitting on them. Too much beer at night may cause a crusty old warrior to roll over in the morning and see something *really* scary, whose name and/or species he can not recall.

When drinking beer, *responsible conduct* is the key! Therefore, Murphy offers his Symptom, Cause, & Solution Guide for warriors who drink beer to enhance the efficiency of their brains:

-- Murphy's Symptom, Cause, & Solution Guide for Warriors Who Drink Beer --

Symptom: Your beer looks crystal clear.
Cause: Bottle is empty. Friends are trying to sober you up.
Solution: Choose your friends more wisely.

Symptom: Your friends look up at you, and laugh.
Cause: You are dancing on a table.
Solution: To avoid a fall, dance in the center.

Symptom: Your feet are squishy, clammy, and *cold*.
Cause: Beer bottle held at an improper angle.
Solution: Point open end of bottle toward ceiling.

Symptom: Your trousers are squishy, clammy, and *warm*.
Cause: Improper bladder control.
Solution: Be patient; in an hour or so, no one will notice.

Symptom: Beer tasteless, stomach cold and wet.
Cause: You missed your mouth with the bottle.
Solution: Go into rest-room, practice in front of mirror.

Symptom: Suddenly you do not recognize anyone.
Cause: You have wandered into the wrong bar.
Solution: Ask if anyone is buying.

Symptom: Your singing voice sounds weak and distorted.
Cause: Beer is too weak, or consumption rate is too low.
Solution: Order two or more beers at a time.

Symptom: Floor appears blurred.
Cause: Looking through the bottom of an empty bottle.
Solution: Induce someone to buy another round.

Symptom: Beer seems tasteless and dry.
Cause: Attempting to drink from an empty bottle.
Solution: (same as above)

Symptom: The *wall* is suddenly covered with fluorescent lights.
Cause: You have fallen *backwards* onto the floor.
Solution: Ask someone to tie you upright to the bar.

Symptom: Your mouth contains four or more cigarette butts.
Cause: You have fallen *forward* onto the floor.
Solution: (same as above)

Symptom: Floor seems to be in front of you, and moving.
Cause: You are being carried out.
Solution: Ask to be carried into another bar.

Symptom: Room seems unusually dark and quiet.
Cause: Bar has closed for the night.
Solution: Sleep on floor, you will awaken when bar reopens.

Symptom: Nose hurts, hands hurt, but your mind is clear.
Cause: You have been in a fight.
Solution: Apologize to your friends, in case it was with them.

Symptom: Walls, floor, ceiling, and friends' faces revolve.
Cause: Beer consumption has exceeded your metabolic limit.
Solution: Cover mouth for twenty minutes or until rotation ceases, whichever occurs first.

Symptom: You do not recall the words to the songs.
Cause: The beer and your consumption rate are *just right*.
Solution: Order another round! Play the air guitar!

If a warrior's beer consumption grossly exceeds his metabolic limit, there is no problem. The floor is usually a convenient and socially accepted refuge, and from a safety standpoint, no one has *ever* fallen off of the floor. Plus, always remember that no one can truthfully claim you are drunk if you can lie on the floor without holding on.

On a safari to Africa, someone forgot the corkscrew, and we had to live on nothing but food and water for three weeks.
[William C. Dukenfield (1880-1946), American humorist, who was better known by his stage name, W.C. Fields]

Murphy's Oaths of Enlistment
for the
Armed Forces

Many centuries ago, in an age before Murphy enlightened the world with his wisdom, warriors swore allegiance to *something*. Usually they pledged eternal loyalty to their military leader: Genghis Kahn, Alexander the Great, or whomever. Later, as the world became ruled by civil authority, warriors swore to defend the King, the Emperor, or the ruling power.

In the early years of the United States, the Armed Forces jointly formulated a generic Oath of Enlistment.   Each person, upon entering military service or upon re-enlisting, was required to take this oath and swear allegiance to a *document*, the Constitution of the United States of America, as follows:

I,_____, do solemnly swear (or affirm) that I will support and defend the Constitution of the United States against all enemies, foreign and domestic; that I will bear true faith and allegiance to the same; and that I will obey the orders of the President of the United States and the orders of the officers appointed over me, according to regulations and the Uniform Code of Military Justice. So help me God.

Big problem! This one-size-fits-all oath never worked. To start with, it was not suited for the Army National Guard and the Air Force National Guard. Warriors in the "Guard" owe allegiance to an individual *state* and to the *Governor* of that state. In an ill-fated attempt to rectify this glaring problem, and to delete reference to the UCMJ, the **National Guard** adopted the following oath:

I, _____, do solemnly swear (or affirm) that I will support and defend the Constitution of the United

States *and the State of* _____
against all enemies, foreign and domestic; that I will bear
true faith and allegiance to the same; and that I will obey the
orders of the President of the United States *and the Governor
of* _____ and the orders of the officers
appointed over me, according to law and regulations. So
help me God.

In recent years the Armed Forces leadership detected fatal flaws
in this system. Because of evolutionary and technological changes
in society, a single oath could never suffice for the Army and the
Navy. The Army's mud-puppies and Navy's squids have nothing
in common from a military viewpoint. Further, the Air Force and
the Marines exist on the extreme opposite ends of the military
cultural spectrum. Each of the four branches of the American
Armed Forces has its own *mission*. Each needs its own oath.
    Fortunately the *philosophy of Murphy* soon solved the dilemma.
Murphy has created four new and unique Oaths of Enlistment, one
for each branch of the Armed Forces:

-- United States Army --

I,_____(printed name of Rambo wannabe),
agree to surrender four (4) years of my mediocre life to the United
States Army because (check one or more):
    ___ I scored too low on the ASVAB to get into the Air Force.
    ___ I am too smart for the Marines.
    ___ I like Navy boats, but I can not swim.
    ___ Other, explain:_____
I fully understand (1) that after completion of the basic sexual
sensitivity training I will be entitled to attend a different Army
school each month, notwithstanding my lack of academic ability
and/or intelligence; (2) that when not in school my "work" hours
will be 1000 to 1500 daily, Monday through Thursday, with time
off for brunch as necessary; (3) that I must make a "good faith"
effort to induce my wife, if any, to stay at home so that she will
not leave me for a smarter Air Force guy or a better looking Sailor;
(4) that for four years I shall be required to claim that I am a mean

green killing machine because my Drill Sergeant will insist that I do so; (5) that I will be promoted to E-7 Bureaucrat within two years; (6) that the only "action" I am likely to see will be a reprimand for sexual harassment; (7) that I should strive to maintain an authoritative appearance even though I am required to accomplish nothing; (8) and that I shall be entitled to wear on my uniform a vast assortment of emblems, crests, badges, patches, and shiny dangling doo-dads in quantities that only a Dollar Store owner can appreciate.

_____(signature of delusional applicant)
****

-- United States Navy --

I,_____(printed name of prospective Swabjockey), instead of completing the remainder of my prison sentence, agree to four (4) years of alternative service in the United States Navy because (check one or more):

____ The Air Force is too intellectual.

____ I want to hang out with Marines without having to *be* one.

____ I enjoy water sports.

____ Other, explain:_____

I fully understand (1) that for four years I must wear clothing that went out of style in the 1960s; (2) that my name will be stenciled on the butt of every pair of trousers that I own, (3) that for some reason I must learn and use a different language than the rest of the English-speaking world; (4) that I may take pride in the fact that all Navy acronyms, rank, insignia, and everything else are different from those of the *real* military services; (5) that when off base I will be mistaken for the Good Humor man in summer, and the Waffen SS in winter; (6) that I must hone my coffee cup handling skills to the point where, aboard a destroyer in a typhoon in 100 foot seas, I will not spill a drop; (7) that I will muster (*whatever that is*) at 1100 each workday unless I am buddy-buddy with the Chief, in which case I may sleep until afternoon soap opera time, and (8) that if I ***do display*** initiative I shall be promoted to Nautical Paint Picker, and that if I ***fail to display*** initiative I shall be cast into the pit with the other dark and slimy squid-like creatures, all of whom shall be banished to the murky depths of the ocean where

normal human beings do not have to associate with them.
_____(signature of prospective parolee)
****

-- United States Marine Corps --

I,_____(printed name of Chesty wannabe), can not read or write. However, I *can* understand the English language if it is *spoken slowly.* I agree to serve four (4) years of my wretched life in the United States Marine Corps because (check one or more):
    ___ I am intimidated by Air Force women.
    ___ I like Navy boats, but I am afraid of soap and water.
    ___ If MASH is reality, the Army is too formal.
    ___ Other, explain:_____
I fully understand (1) that for four years my lack of intelligence will be considered a great virtue; (2) that I must shout unintelligible animal noises for 14 hours per day; (3) that **"Kill, Sir!"** will be the correct answer to any and all questions from my superiors; (4) that being called a Jarhead (*whatever that is*) is a great honor, and that "Uncle Sam's Misguided Children" is a statement of fact; (5) that I will be stationed in the worst cesspools of the known world; (6) that I shall renounce all right to *think* (if capable of thinking) for the duration of my enlistment; (7) that throughout my enlistment I must drink, brawl, kick cats, sing obscene songs, embellish War Stories beyond recognition, and corrupt members of the opposite sex; (8) that I must go anywhere at any time and destroy whatever or whomever I am ordered to destroy; and (9) that if, for any reason, I am discharged or go AWOL prior to the expiration of my enlistment, I agree to voluntarily return to the psychiatric hospital from which I escaped.
_____("X" or "thumb print" of Montezuma boy)
****

-- United States Air Force --

I,_____(printed name of Zoomie applicant), being incapable of finding a job in the private sector, eagerly look forward to enjoying four (4) years of leisure in the United States Air Force because (check one or more):

___ I am too smart for the Army.

___ I am too delicate for the Marines.

___ The Navy is too corporate.

___ Other, explain:_____

For four years of my worthless life I fully understand (1) that after completing basic training (*snicker*) I will be known as a lean, mean, donut-eating chairborne ranger; (2) that I may address my peers and superiors by their first names because we are not *really* in a military service; (3) that I may sit behind a desk and take credit for all work, if any, done by others; (4) that I should make a good-faith effort to clean my knife before stabbing the next person in the back; (5) that I may remain flaccid and avoid all forms of demeaning physical exercise and/or exertion, exclusive of the annual two minute bike-riding PT test; (6) that I will never be exposed to any form of danger or threat of violence or physical harm; (7) that if I ever have to wear anything except civvies, it will be a spiffy blue uniform fashioned after that of a Greyhound bus driver; and (8) that my sole responsibility is to claim that I support and defend the Constitution of the United States (even though I believe myself to be *above* all of that).

_____(signature of wild-blue-yonder-wonder)

****

Nobody ever died of laughter, and not a shred of evidence favors the idea that life should be taken seriously.

Murphy's Introduction
to
Redneck Warriors

Warriors come in two versions: ***Regular*** and ***Redneck***. Neither is necessarily good or bad, they are just *different*. One version speaks Regular English, the other speaks Redneck English. Plus, there are broad cultural differences between the two species.

The elite cream of American youth, the top ten percent, grows up to become warriors. Most of these professional assassins will be ***Regular Warriors***, but some will be ***Redneck Warriors***. It is imperative, therefore, that each professional warrior be able to categorize each of his brothers-in-arms as either a Regular Warrior or a Redneck Warrior.

In combat there is no difference between the Regular and the Redneck variants, for both are equally lethal. But in an off-base social environment they exhibit a host of differences. If these differences are not thoroughly understood, communication and unit cohesion will suffer.

Regular Warriors must learn to appreciate the culture and values of their Redneck Warrior compatriots. Only then can they bond together as the world's most fearsome fighting team. To assist all professional warriors in this endeavor, Murphy has identified the unique characteristics of the ***off-base*** Redneck Warrior.

No Redneck Warrior can possess *all* of the socio-economic beliefs, habits, and traits enumerated below by Murphy. Yet, if a warrior can truthfully answer "yes" to at least 30 percent of the following statements, he is a certified Redneck Warrior according to Murphy's scientific cultural analysis profile. In the interest of clarity, these statements are grouped in seven categories:

1. Social Enigmas and the Redneck Warrior
2. Home Life and the Redneck Warrior
3. Sex and the Redneck Warrior
4. "Forbidden Fruit" and the Redneck Warrior

5. Education and the Redneck Warrior
6. Motor Vehicles and the Redneck Warrior
7. Personal Hygiene and the Redneck Warrior

-- Social Enigmas and the Redneck Warrior --

You have been thrown out of the zoo for heckling the monkeys.

You think the moon landings were *faked*, but you believe the TV wrestling shows are *real*.

At the carnival you had your photograph taken with a "Freak of Nature," but your friends can not tell which is which.

You are amazed that gas stations keep their rest-rooms so clean.

You think people "out of your league" bowl on a different night.

You need to have only a few more holes punched in your card to get a freebie at the local Tattoo Parlor.

In your church the organist avoids the high notes so the dogs on the floor will not start howling.

In your church the treasurer refuses to buy a chandelier until someone claims they can play one.

You routinely "make change" in the church offering plate.

You wonder why the stock market has no fence around it.

You always find "ammo" on your mother's Christmas wish list.

You have no reason to buy a program at stock car races.

Your lifetime ambition is to own a fireworks stand.

When you give directions to your home, you always include the phrase, "After you turn off of the paved road . . . ."

You named your male children after Confederate Army generals.

You think that going on a cruise with your spouse means driving around the parking lot at McDonalds.

You have left a six-pack of beer in the casket with the deceased.

At least half of the time you come home from the garbage dump with more than you left with.

Two or more members of your immediate family have died after shouting, "Hey, guys, watch this!"

You have two or more relatives named Bubba or Junior.

Someone in your family is named Rufus or Cletus.

-- Home Life and the Redneck Warrior --

Originally, your coffee table was a CATV cable reel.

Your Halloween pumpkin has more teeth than you have.

You let your 16 year old daughter smoke at the dinner table, in front of her children.

Both your spouse and your daughter keep their spit cups on the dining room table.

You have recorded 50 or more episodes of *The Dukes of Hazzard*.

You refuse to watch the Emmy Awards because *Hee-Haw* never got the critical acclaim it deserved.

Your functional TV sits on top of your non-functional TV.

A guest once lit a match in your living room, and your whole home exploded right off of its wheels.

You consider possum to be "the other white meat."

There is a stuffed possum *somewhere* in your home.

Two or more of your children were delivered on a pool table.

You were *shooting* pool when one of your children was born.

You think a "loaded dishwasher" refers to a drunk wife.

Your spouse keeps the stuff from Graceland on the coffee table.

Your spouse's dress shoes are four ply non-skid Red Wings.

Your best salad bowls all have *Miracle Whip* printed on them.

You and your coon dogs have the same favorite front-yard tree.

Two or more of your coon dogs perished in the rubble when your front or back porch collapsed.

You have been in a marital custody battle over a coon dog.

Your coon dogs and your wallet are *all* on chains.

You think the annual Thanksgiving dinner is the perfect time for your "pull my finger" trick.

While cutting the grass at home, you have found a lost truck.

You believe that "taking out the trash" means taking your live-in mother-in-law to watch Friday night wrestling.

Your children took your siphon hose to Show & Tell.

There is a framed diploma on your living room wall with a filled-in blank space, followed by the words, "Truck Driving School."

Smith & Wesson and Redman send you Christmas cards.

You do not own any shirt that has no logo on it.

You have not removed the "Wide Load" sign from your home.

-- Sex and the Redneck Warrior --

You hooked up with your girlfriend after finding her name and number on the rest-room stall door at the truck stop.

You think that women are turned on by your expertise at making seductive animal noises.

Your biggest turn-on is your girlfriend's beer belly.

Nonetheless, you believe that watching professional wrestling on TV is the *ultimate* form of foreplay.

You make sure the parking brake is set before making love.

While making love, cigarettes are a no-no, but *smokeless* is OK.

If you ever engage in conversation while making love, it is usually just to say, "Don't worry, ain't no cars coming!"

When making love, you routinely economize by using lard.

You think "safe sex" is a padded dashboard.

You think Genitalia is the national airline of Italy.

-- "Forbidden Fruit" and the Redneck Warrior --

You can not marry your girlfriend because you would go to jail.

Your brother-in-law is also your favorite uncle.

You consider family reunions as the ideal place to pick up hot women, and maybe even find Miss Right.

You lurk under the mistletoe at Christmas and wait for your sister or your hot-to-trot aunt, Susie-Mae, to wander by.

You remarry, but you still have the same in-laws.

Your father's will leaves all of his assets to his girlfriend, but she can not get the money until she turns 16.

In your church the congregation has four or fewer surnames.

One or more of the women in your family has claimed that her pregnancy was the result of an alien abduction.

You have a gene pool, *sort of,* but it has no deep end.

You have a five-generation family tree -- with no branches.

You believe that incest is OK if you keep it in the family.

-- Education and the Redneck Warrior --

Fourth Grade was the best three years of your life.

In the 7th Grade you dated your father's current wife.

You claim the 8th Grade in Junior High as your senior year.

The school set up a day-care center for your Junior High prom.

Your Junior High theme song was "Friends in Low Places."

You are considered to be the local authority on ways to sneak liquor into Junior High sporting events.

You stare at the grape-juice bottle because it says, "Concentrate."

-- Motor Vehicles and the Redneck Warrior --

You "totaled" over 75 percent of the vehicles you have owned.

You have been featured on TV five or more times to describe your miraculous survival in yet another car wreck.

Your *home* is mobile, but most of your *vehicles* are not.

You have at least three vehicles up on blocks in your yard.

You know how many bales of hay your spouse's car will hold.

The only truck you can drive is so old that its Blue Book value depends on how much gas is in it.

The tailgate of your truck is held closed with bungee cords.

Your truck has a two-tone paint job: primer red and primer gray.

The rear tires on your truck are twice as wide as the front tires.

At best, your truck is worth one-tenth of the value of your coon dogs that ride in it.

Your truck has a shop rag where the gas cap should be.

You have repainted your truck with a brush and house paint.

Your home does not have shades or curtains, but your truck does.

You treasure your personalized license plate because it was made by your father when he was "gone for a few years."

You think the final line of the National Anthem is, "Gentleman, start your engines!"

You never need to pull off at a Rest Stop on the highway as long as you keep those empty milk jugs handy.

-- Personal Hygiene and the Redneck Warrior --

You include "chiggers" on your list of top three health concerns.

The Salvation Army rejected all of your old clothes.

You keep two cans of *Raid* on the dining room table.

For an hour you can entertain yourself with a fly swatter.

You use flea & tick soap during each end-of-the-month bath.

However, you must skip the annual end-of-December bath (the tub will be full of beer and ice for the party).

You need shoes and a flashlight to go to the rest-room at night.

Your coon dogs gag each time they watch you eat.

Because of your *appearance*, you have been fired from your job on the garbage truck.

Conscientiously, you always pull up your jeans and tighten your belt when you see posters that announce, "Say No to Crack!"

Your wife's toilet bowl brush doubles as your back-scratcher.

You think a bubble bath is the result of eating too many beans.

All Redneck Warriors -- those who truthfully answered "yes" to at least 30 percent of the above-listed statements -- have now been positively identified. Murphy cautions each such person that their values, beliefs, and culture may not be fully understood by some of their Regular Warrior brothers-in-arms. For Redneck Warriors, this can be a source of social friction which may adversely affect interpersonal relationships. Many times in social settings, Redneck Warriors may be considered uncouth.

Consequently, Redneck Warriors should accept the advice of the world's foremost expert. Murphy recommends that you make a good-faith attempt to be considerate when socializing with Regular Warriors and their families. If you follow Murphy's suggestions, below, you will minimize the chance of grossing-out your Regular Warrior associates:

-- Murphy's Social Graces for Redneck Warriors --

Your dogs should not be allowed to eat at the table until after all guests have finished their meal.

Chitlins should not be the main course for your dinner guests.

When your coon dog falls in love with a guest's leg, courtesy demands that you give them a little privacy.

When expecting overnight guests, your coon dogs should vacate the guest bedroom for the evening.

After your dogs vacate the guest bedroom, you should vacuum the sheets *before* your guests arrive.

The centerpiece on your dining room table should not be the work product of a taxidermist.

Never attempt to urinate from a moving truck that is carrying guests, especially if you are driving.

Dim your headlights for oncoming vehicles, even when a round is chambered and the deer is just standing there.

Remember to say "I'm sorry" after throwing up in a friend's car.

When you send your guest's wife down the road with a gas can, it is unwise to push your luck by asking her to bring back beer, too.

It is uncouth to lay rubber when in a funeral procession.

Although they are uncomfortable, shoes and socks must be worn to all weddings, formal or informal.

Hunting dogs and livestock are unsuitable as wedding gifts.

Rat-traps, although practical, make uncouth wedding gifts.

If you are the groom, it is unwise to bring a date to the wedding.

A woman should not wear a tube-top or hair rollers to a formal church wedding if she is the bride.

For wedding photographs, remove the toothpick from your mouth.

When dancing at wedding receptions, refrain from removing your partner's undergarments, regardless of the temperature.

When with guests, do not fish coins out of urinals.

Leave beer coolers closed during all church services.

Children should refrain from using tobacco products while inside of the church or on the church grounds.

Generally speaking, it is unwise to ask the State Trooper to hold your beer while you search for your driver's license.

It is counterproductive to drink a beer during a job interview.

To avoid a potentially awkward situation with guests, go to all public rest-rooms in town and scratch your sister's name out of messages that begin, "For a good time, call . . . ."

When dining with a guest in a restaurant, **never** place your white styrofoam *spit* cup near your guest's white styrofoam *drink* cup (be forewarned and *trust Murphy* on this one!).

Murphy's Laws of
Lust, Sex, & Seduction
for Warriors

Warriors, beware! All of the good ones are taken. And if a good one *is not* taken, there is a good reason.

Once upon a time the world of the professional warrior was the exclusive province of men. But in this modern enlightened age there is a growing number of gung-ho women warriors out there, too. Yet, a stern note of caution: when Murphy speaks of women warriors, he means the ***real women warriors*** -- not the sniveling insecure feminist weaklings.

Although a *real* woman warrior can be as lethal in combat as her male counterpart, men and women are not the same species. For one thing, their social philosophies differ. For the uneducated, Murphy explains the social ethos of the two sexes:

> **Male Warrior social ethos**: It is great to be a man! At conception you had a fifty-fifty chance, but you made it. Now the entire world is your private urinal. Wrinkles give you character. You only have to shave from the neck up. And when you drop by to see your friends, you bring along a six-pack of beer, not some cutesy little wrapped gift.

> Unlike women, you know that two pair of shoes is more than enough. You follow the Blue Light Special and get an eight-pack of underwear for $4.95, and hair stylists and dry cleaners will never try to rob you blind. If you happen to stumble into the deep and dark snake-pit of marriage, at least you get to keep your last name. You are a fighter, a brawler, a killer, the best America has to offer. You are a male warrior, and men can do anything.

> **Female Warrior social ethos**: It is great to be a woman! You joined the Armed Forces because you wanted to break

things and hurt people. You love the smell of cordite in the morning. Here you enjoy the company of reckless warriors with a lethal mindset. You open your own doors, you buy your own drinks, and you despise the *politically correct* mentality of social weaklings.

You hold the pathetic hand-wringing feminist whiny-babies in contempt. You prefer the heady aura of Hoppe's No. 9 Nitro Powder Solvent over perfume, warpaint over lip-gloss, combat boots over high heels, *Guns & Ammo* over the tabloids. Off duty you are a sexual predator without equal, and proud of it. You can hold your own and carouse, curse, drink, lie, and fight with the world's best. You are a female warrior, and women can do anything.

In love and war, "nice" warriors *really* finish last. Consequently, when it comes to sex and seduction, lust and love, Murphy has excellent advice. All red-blooded warriors, both men and women, will profit from Murphy's time-tested knowledge of the erotic arts. In the amorous game of life, he knows the rules. Murphy cautions all crazed wild-eyed feminist zealots to read the "**Notice**" on page vii, because his rules are not for you. Murphy's rules are for the *real* warriors, both men and women. <u>Murphy offers them from the</u> ***<u>male point of view</u>***. <u>For women warriors, this is</u> ***<u>no problem</u>***. Just mentally transpose Murphy's gender verbiage and apply his logic. These eternal truths are divided into six sub-chapters:

1. The Game of Sex and Seduction.
2. Warriors, Beware!
3. Living with a Woman.
4. Could It Be Love?
5. The Dark Snakepit of Marriage.
6. The Woman Warrior's Unique Point of View.

-- The Game of Sex and Seduction --

In the game of seduction, if you want to hit the jackpot, you have to drop a few quarters into the slot.

Money can not really buy love. Nonetheless, it *can* get you into an excellent bargaining position.

Although money can not actually buy love, it can *rent* it.

The best women are free -- and worth every penny of it.

Anything worth doing is worth doing for money.

When it comes to the honored and age-old art of seduction, candy is dandy, but liquor is quicker.

There are many mechanical devices which increase sexual arousal, such as the Mercedes-Benz SL55 AMG convertible.

It is not pre-marital sex if you do not intend to get married.

Sex is like air; it is most important when you are not getting any.

Do not worry, it only seems kinky the first time.

Sex is dirty only when it is done *exactly* right.

No matter how much you get, it is never enough. There is no remedy for sex except more sex. Never say no!

Enough is never enough! Everything in excess! Take big bites!

No matter how many times you have had it, if it is available, take it, because it will never be exactly the same again.

There may be a few (*very* few) things better than sex, but there is nothing exactly like it.

Sow your wild oats, then pray for crop failure.

Never fear! No warrior has ever created a baby in one month by sleeping with nine women.

Do it only with the best. Bad girls make good company.

The younger, the better. Only wine improves with age.

If it is not erotic, it is not interesting, and sex has no calories.

Abstain from wine, women, and song -- mostly song.

Warriors, it is better to copulate than never.

Chastity is *not* hereditary, and it can be cured.

Sex *is* hereditary (if your parents never had it, neither will you).

If you never procreate, neither will your children.

Sex appeal is 10 percent what you have and 90 percent what a woman thinks you have.

Always tell her she is beautiful -- especially if she is not.

The more beautiful the woman is, the easier it is to leave her with no hard feelings.

Nonetheless, *all* women are beautiful when the lights go out.

If *she* feels good, do it, for a man is only as old as the woman he feels (*think* about it).

Sex is one of the nine reasons for reincarnation. The other eight reasons are not important.

What matters is not the length of the wand, but the magic.

A vasectomy is never having to say you are sorry.

A dress that zips up the back is usually the most reliable harbinger of an amorous evening.

A woman fond of zippers should *never* live alone.

The simple formula for an amorous evening: scratch her back.

The main problem with trying to resist temptation is the knowledge that it may never pass your way again.

With a voluptuous and sensuous woman, the only surefire way to get rid of temptation is to yield to it.

Children in the back seat cause few accidents. But accidents in the back seat cause a *lot* of children.

Three simple rules for life: (1) Never eat at a place called Mom's. (2) Never play cards with a man called Doc. (3) Never sleep with a woman crazier than you are.

Whoever coined the term *necking* did not understand anatomy.

In the game of seduction, lust does not *really* make the world go around, but it makes the ride exciting.

All women should be encouraged to use what Mother Nature gave them before Father Time takes it away.

The game of seduction is never called off on account of darkness.

Only young children, fools, and old reprobates sneer at lust.

-- Warriors, Beware! --

When it comes to women, seeing can be deceiving.

A woman's beauty invites a man's folly.

Unfortunately, warriors rarely lust after women they can afford.

When with a woman, a warrior's head is the dupe of his heart.

Romance discriminates against the meek and cautious.

The probability of meeting a seductive, beautiful, and receptive woman increases by pyramidal progression when you are in the company of a better looking or richer male friend.

Avoid frigid women (although they often put on the best show).

A wise warrior never meets a woman, for the first time, in light so dim that he can not read a newspaper.

You can usually determine when a woman is not telling a man the truth. You can see her lips moving.

A rabid skunk is better company than a woman with scruples.

Any woman incapable of passion, or not inclined toward amorous conduct, should be shot on sight.

It was not the *apple* on the tree, it was the *pair* on the ground, that started all of the trouble in the Garden.

Every woman worries about pregnancy. Unfortunately she does not always worry at the right time.

The only time any woman ever wished she was a year older is when she was pregnant.

Absence makes the heart grow fonder -- of someone else.

With women, availability is a function of time. The minute a warrior gets interested is usually the same minute that a richer and better looking warrior comes along.

Avoid the fatal "he came, he saw, she conquered" syndrome.

The more a warrior learns about women, the more he yearns for the company of a loyal old dog.

Beware of liquor! It can make you shoot at women -- and miss!

-- Living with a Woman --

Love is blind, but living with a woman is a genuine eye-opener.

Life with a woman is not a journey, but a predicament.

The woman who is easy to get is usually hard to take.

The trouble with women is that they lack the power of conversation, but not the power of speech.

Women speak in four tenses: (1) past tense, (2) present tense, (3) future tense, and (4) pretense.

Women go on talking, not knowing how to get off.

Warriors prefer women who wag their tails, not their tongues.

Given a chance, the enemy will kill you quickly. But a woman takes her time.

Women may forgive and forget -- but they *never* forget.

Women are "generous to a fault" when it is *their* fault.

When dealing with a woman, a warrior usually should tell her the truth (unless, of course, he is a talented liar).

There are two sure-fire ways to explain complex technological issues to a woman, but neither has ever worked.

In the overall scheme of things, sex takes the least amount of time and causes the greatest amount of trouble.

Women who always "sleep like a baby" will never have one.

Always be sincere with a woman, even when you have to fake it.

An honorable warrior never hits a woman unless she deserves it.

Cassandra did not get half the beating that she deserved.

In order of preference, men like (1) dogs, (2) beer, and (3) wide screen TVs. An *exceptional* woman *may* sneak into the top ten.

Men prefer loyal dogs because, unlike women, dogs do not whine unless something is *really* wrong.

The primary difference between a (1) whining woman at the back door and a (2) whining dog at the back door is that -- if you let them both inside -- the dog will quit whining.

. . . Murphy's Top Ten Rules for women who live with a man:

1.   Learn to work the toilet seat. Men need it up. You need it down. If it is up, put it down. You can do it if you try.

2.   If you want something, **ask** for it! Speak English! Routine hints will not work. Strong hints will not work.

3.   Unless our home is on fire, speak only during commercials.

4.   If a man asks you what is wrong, and you say "nothing," the conversation is over. Learn to live with it.

5.   If you have a *problem*, men offer solutions. If you are looking for sympathy, call your girlfriends.

6.   If you think that you are fat, maybe you are. Never ask. Men are smart enough not to answer.

7.   You have enough clothes.

8.   You have far too many shoes.

9.   Men understand only the three basic colors, like computer default settings. *Pumpkin* is a fruit, not a color. *Peach* is also a fruit. And whatever *mauve* may be, it is not a color.

10. Do not pout, do not sulk, do not whine, and do not cry.

-- Could It Be Love? --

A warrior can not buy love, but he will pay heavily for it.

Love is the triumph of imagination over intelligence.

Love is the cruel delusion that one woman differs from another.

There is no difference between a (1) wise man and (2) an absolute fool if they fall in love.

Love is an *ideal* thing. Lust is a *real* thing. Confusing the two always brings disaster.

Never confuse lust and love. Lust is a matter of physics. Love is a matter of chemistry.

Lust and love, although different, both require an accomplice.

A warrior can be happy with any woman if he does not love her.

Warriors who fall in love usually have to climb out.

Love is blind. If Jack is in love, he is no judge of Jill's beauty.

When love wears thin, faults grow thick.

Those who are sensible about love are incapable of it.

Platonic love exists only from the neck up.

If a warrior refuses to lie to a woman in love, he has little consideration for her feelings.

In many instances, religion has done lust a great favor by proclaiming it to be a sin.

If a warrior feels nauseous and tingly all over, he is either (1) in love, or he (2) has smallpox. Both have dire consequences.

-- The Dark Snakepit of Marriage --

The institution of marriage has been around throughout recorded history. Centuries ago the marital union was simple. If a man and a woman consensually lived together, they were "married."

The first real trouble started in the English Parliament in 1753. Lord Hardwicke's Act required a (1) "banns or license" and a (2) ceremony by the Church of England before a man and a woman could live together. No problem; many hot-to-trot couples went to nearby Scotland where only "mutual consent" was required for cohabitation. Nonetheless, Lord Hardwicke and his edict signaled the birth of *government intervention* in marriage. Sadly, the days of happy marriage were truly numbered.

In the new United States, things started off well. In 1809 the New York legislature was the first to officially endorse "common law" marriage. In New York, mutual consent and cohabitation became sufficient to create a legal union.

Nonetheless, the Twentieth Century brought sheer disaster. A married man and woman became entangled in an intricate and inextricable web of rights and obligations created by law. These entanglements transformed marriage into a suffocating *penal* institution. Those who dared to try to escape faced community property battles, child custody disputes, the albatross of alimony, and civil sanctions without end. Murphy offers unique advice for the unfortunate souls who may be tempted to get married:

A bachelor looks before he leaps -- and does not leap.

The only happy people are (1) married women and (2) bachelors.

Bachelors know more about women than married men. Otherwise, bachelors would be married men, too.

It has been said that a warrior is incomplete until he gets married, but after that, of course, he is finished.

A warrior will never experience true joy and happiness until after he gets married. Then it is too late.

In *theory*, love is never having to say you are sorry. In *reality*, marriage is never having a chance to say anything.

A married man's home is his hassle.

A warrior may be a fool and not know it -- unless he is married.

A husband is what is left of a married man after his spirit dies.

Marriage is a lottery. But when you lose, you must keep the ticket.

Sooner or later every married man will believe in Hell -- on Earth.

All marriages are bliss for about a week. It is the living together *afterward* that will be Hell on Earth.

Successful marriage, *if* there were such a thing, would require (1) a blind wife and (2) a deaf husband.

With a woman, marriage is only a brief suspension of hostilities.

For warriors, marriage is an evil institution that equates to slavery.

For a warrior, a golden ring on the third finger is about as bad as an iron ring through the nose.

For a warrior, marriage is like taking a bath -- it usually is not so hot once you get accustomed to it.

Marriage is a process by which the grocer gets the florist's account.

Tragically, warriors often marry the person who is most available when they are the most vulnerable.

A groom is a man with his last chance of happiness behind him.

Before his liver fails, a warrior can never drink enough of his mother-in-law's booze to get even.

In a government study, 92 percent of married people did not want their mother-in-law within two day's driving distance.

A woman never forgets where she went on her honeymoon. A man often forgets where, but never *why*.

An ex-girlfriend is just a memory, but an ex-wife is forever.

Lust is a quest, marriage is a conquest, divorce is an inquest.

Love is grand. Divorce is a hundred grand.

Nonetheless, in marriage a horrible ending is always *much* better than horrors without end.

-- The Woman Warrior's Unique Point of View --

A smart woman warrior knows that men -- like coffee and chocolate -- are much better if they are rich.

A woman warrior prefers a man who has something tender about him, as long as it is *legal* tender.

True, all work and no play makes Jack a dull boy. But it makes Jill an exceptionally rich widow.

A woman's greatest labor saving device is a rich husband.

Behind every rich husband is a woman with nothing to wear.

A woman warrior knows that a man should never argue with her when she is tired -- or rested.

There are two sides to every argument -- unless one of the parties to the argument is a woman.

If a man ever argues with a woman, and it turns out that he is right, he should apologize at once.

Men should never try to out-stubborn a woman.

Women warriors pick their men -- *to pieces*.

When a woman wants a man's opinion, she gives it to him.

The qualities a woman initially finds attractive in a man are the same ones she despises six months later.

A smart woman warrior never appeals to a man's better nature. She knows that most men do not have one.

Love is a matter of chemistry, which explains why most women warriors treat men as toxic waste.

For an aggressive female sexual predator on the prowl, sex is like the falling snow (if you do not know the pithy little analogy that proves this axiom, too bad).

If and when a woman ever *finally* understands her man, she stops listening to him.

Women and cats will do as they please. Men and dogs should relax and get accustomed to it.

Murphy's Analysis
of
"Politically Correct" Disease

"Politically Correct" Disease is a social illness. Those afflicted are a motley assortment of interpersonal cripples, non-achievers, liberal whiny-babies, and misfits. There is no known cure.

Politically Correct people constitute a festering sore on the face of society. These hand-wringing parasites, these weaklings, have drifted out of touch with reality. Each day they try to pattern their lives around a warm and fuzzy notion of *fairness* and *inclusion*. They offer nothing, build nothing, contribute nothing of substance. These liberal purveyors of psycho-babble try nothing, risk nothing, gain nothing. To the detriment of all concerned, they simply whine about the *unfairness* of society.

Although the essence of Politically Correct Disease is frustrating to define, it is easy to identify. Consider the following example:

Situation: You are walking down the street with your girlfriend and your three small children. Without warning a deranged man, brandishing a huge knife, begins shouting obscenities and running toward you. You have a loaded Smith & Wesson .44 Magnum pistol (think, *Dirty Harry* and *"Make my day!"*) in your hand. You have three seconds before the crazed lunatic -- now screaming, "Kill! Kill! Kill!" -- reaches you, your girlfriend, and your children. What should you do?

The "Politically Correct" response: This is unfair! There is not enough information to answer the question. Is the deranged man poor or oppressed? Is he a member of a minority group? Is he financially or culturally disadvantaged? Has anyone treated him badly or provoked him? Has anyone acted toward him in a discriminatory manner?

Maybe I can swing my gun like a club and knock the knife out of the man's hand. Can I do this without hurting his hand?

Perhaps I can run fast enough to get away. If so, will the man feel less anger toward only my girlfriend and children?

If I don't resist, there is the possibility that the man will be satisfied with killing only me. But maybe he doesn't intend to kill anyone. Maybe he simply wants to *wound* us. Or, perhaps he doesn't want to hurt anyone; maybe he's just having a bad day and wants to *scare* us. Maybe it's a fake knife.

Maybe my appearance or clothing represents an ethnic insult to the man. If so, do I have time to apologize? Will he think I am sincere? If not, and if the man does intend to kill me, perhaps I can grab him and hold on. Could my girlfriend and children get away while I am being stabbed to death?

If I dropped my gun, would the man feel less threatened? On the other hand, if I fired my gun into the air, might it induce the man to reconsider his antisocial conduct? Or would it create a greater provocation? And to what extent might it endanger low-flying birds which might be on an endangered species list?

There are too many unknowns! I need time to talk this over with my spiritual advisor, my attorney, my psychiatrist, and my friends. Then I can decide on a non-discriminatory course of action which will be fair to all concerned.

The Warrior's response: Shoot him. If he's still twitching after he hits the ground, shoot him again.

Then we'll go to a ball game, sing the National Anthem, pig out on hot dogs and popcorn and soda pop, and be thankful for another day of freedom.

As opposed to pathetic Politically Correct cripples, American Warriors are easy to identify. First of all, American Warriors are gun nuts. In their homes you will find dozens of back issues of *American Rifleman*, *Shotgun News*, *Gun Digest*, and such.

American Warriors watch the wars in Kuwait and Afghanistan and Iraq on TV, and they always wish they could be there to police up the empty brass. A warrior's wife and his girlfriend both think that his aura of Hoppe's No. 9 is his favorite after-shave lotion. And when a warrior passes a magazine rack, he checks out the cover of *Playboy* -- after reading *Guns & Ammo* page by page.

A warrior's children are usually life members of the NRA. Each month a warrior spends more money on ammo than on food. Look behind his house and you will find more empty .50 caliber ammo cans than they stock at the local Army Reserve armory. And when it comes to knives, rifles, and machineguns, warriors have enough to equip a couple of platoons. Plus, they have bayonets for rifles they do not yet own.

Warriors know that guns and guts made America free, and they intend to keep it that way. They know that "gun control" efforts are not about *guns*. They are about *control* by liberal communist pinko pacifists whose vision of a socialist utopian neverland can not possibly exist anywhere in the real world. They know that you have only the rights you are willing to fight for, and they know:

If you do not know your rights, you do not have any.

Warriors and free men do not ask permission to bear arms.

What part of "shall not be infringed" do liberals not understand?

An armed man is a citizen. An unarmed man is a subject.

Criminals love gun control -- it makes their job much safer.

Dialing "911" is simply government sponsored dial-a-prayer.

A gun in hand is far better than a policeman on the phone.

Each day, 87,976,374 gun owners kill no one except criminals.

Politicians who believe that guns cause crime also believe that (1) matches cause arson, and (2) pencils cause misspelled words.

Guns have only two enemies, (1) rust and (2) ignorant politicians.

Know guns, know peace and safety; *no* guns, no peace or safety.

Unlike pitiful Politically Correct wimps, American Warriors are zealous patriots who are obsessed with freedom, family values, and the work ethic. They collectively form society's sword and shield against the forces of crime and evil. They are society's doers, workers, achievers, entrepreneurs, adventurers, planners, and leaders. Many have framed photographs of Teddy Roosevelt in their homes, for they live by his ***Daring Greatly*** philosophy:

It is **not the critic** who counts, not the man who points out how the strong man stumbled, or where the doer of deeds could have done them better.

The credit belongs to **the warrior** who is actually in the arena, the warrior whose face is marred by dust and sweat and blood, the warrior who strives valiantly, the warrior who errs and comes up short again and again. Credit belongs to the warrior who knows the great enthusiasms, the great devotions, and spends himself in a worthy cause.

The credit belongs to **the warrior** who -- at the best -- knows in the end the triumphs of high achievement. Credit belongs to the warrior who -- at the worst -- if he fails, at least fails while ***Daring Greatly***. His place shall never be with those cold and timid souls who know neither defeat nor victory.

[when quoting Roosevelt, above, Murphy has substituted *"the warrior"* where Roosevelt said *"the man"*]

All red-blooded American Warriors should pity the mindless rabble infected with Politically Correct Disease. They should *honor* the warriors, for it is America's Warriors who must beware of people like Norman M. Thomas, who once opined:

The American people will never knowingly adopt socialism. But if we can deceive them with liberalism, they will soon adopt every fragment of the socialist program, until one day America will be a socialist nation -- without knowing how it happened.

[Norman M. Thomas (1884-1968), socialist, pacifist, editor of the leftist *Nation* newspaper, six times the Socialist Party candidate for U.S. President (1928, 1932, 1936, 1940, 1944, 1948), and co-founder of the American Civil Liberties Union in 1917]

Murphy's Guide
to
Politicians and Government

In the beginning, all was well. No politicians! No governments! Anarchy reigned throughout the world, and professional warriors controlled society. Life was good!

Then things began to go downhill. When he wrote *Republic*, Plato (c 427-347 BC) theorized that mankind needed a socialist utopia. He hoped for a society ruled not by the sword, but by non-warriors who were "more qualified" to administer functions of state. Aristotle (c 384-322 BC), in a fit of lunacy, dreamed up the concept of "democracy." He wanted a system wherein the rabble (the ignorant majority) would choose a civil ruler.

Warriors of the day simply should have lopped off the heads of Plato and Aristotle to squelch the "democracy movement" in the bud. Tragically the warriors failed to do so, and society has been on a fast track to disaster ever since.

Today we are burdened with civil control, which begat *public officials*: the most sleazy, devious, self-serving, back-stabbing life forms on planet Earth. *Politics* is defined as the process by which public officials are chosen. All of these public officials have only one money-grubbing goal -- to *remain* public officials. They are called *politicians*, although the words (1) scoundrel, (2) parasite, (3) liar, and (4) scalawag would be more accurate.

Politicians created the evil concept of *government* to maintain power and control, so that they can continue to enrich themselves at the expense of the governed. Until the world gets so bad that professional warriors have to rise up and rid the Earth of all politicians and government, we are stuck with them. Therefore, Murphy offers the following eternal truths for warriors:

Public Office is the final refuge of the incompetent.

To succeed in politics, one must rise above his principles.

The difference between a politician and a snail is that a snail leaves his slime behind.

No politician can afford to be just a *little* crooked.

Politicians are *sneaks* in the grass.

For politicians, hypocrisy is the Vaseline of social intercourse.

The only correct way to look at a politician is down.

The territory in a politician's rhetoric is mined with equivocation.

The only goal of all politicians is simply to get re-elected.

A politician's ethics are as temporary as today's newspaper.

Victory goes to the rich politician who spends enough money to convince the poor that he is on their side.

Whenever any virtuous and worthy cause of the people is entrusted to politicians, it is forever lost.

Those who can, *do*.
   -- Those who can not do, *teach*.
   -- Those who can not teach, *administer*.
   -- Those who can not administer, work for the *government*.

Government bureaucracy defends the status quo long after the quo has lost its status.

It is impossible to visually determine whether the bureaucrats are sitting on their hands, or covering their butts, or both.

A bureaucrat's desk is his castle -- and his parking space.

The purpose of a government bureaucracy is to perpetuate itself.

All actions and decisions within a bureaucracy are for the purpose of keeping the bureaucracy intact.

If there is a hidden way to delay a crucial decision, some efficient government bureaucrat will always find it.

A taxpayer is someone who never took a Civil Service Exam, but who still works for the government.

Taxes are contributions which do not benefit the taxed.

Government expands to absorb all tax revenue -- and then some.

Regardless of the need or the budget restraints, government will continue to grow at a rate of 14 percent per year.

Those who wish to understand government should not waste time reading the Constitution. Instead, they should read each entry in the "Government Offices" section of the Washington phone book.

The legislature, when in session, is more dangerous than a deranged and intoxicated homicidal teenage maniac with a chain saw.

No man's life, liberty, or property is safe while the legislature or congress is in session.

When government compromises, the result is inevitably more expensive than either of the original proposals.

If there is no law now, there soon will be.

Proliferation of new laws begets proliferation of new loopholes.

In government, bad regulation begets worse regulation.

In government, common sense begets nonsense.

In government, bad procedures are supplemented, never repealed.

The quality of new legislation is *inversely* proportional to the degree of mindless media clamor that prompted it.

In a government project the extent of public benefit is *inversely* proportional to the cost of the project.

In government, accomplishment is *inversely* proportional to the amount of paper used.

In government, the higher the level, the greater the confusion.

In government, growth breeds complexity, which breeds decay.

In government, neurosis is communicable.

The two grammatical criteria for all government mandates:
1. Never use one word when a dozen will suffice.
2. If the mandate still can be understood, it is not complete.

All government mandates must be worded so as to be totally incomprehensible to the governed.

All government specifications must be expressed in the least understood terms, such as "furlongs per fortnight."

The sole purpose of a government memorandum is to protect the memorandum writer.

No government project is ever on schedule or within budget.

An elephant is merely a mouse, built to government specifications.

When government does something that could have been done differently, it usually would have been better if it had.

If there is anything on Earth that a Public Servant hates to do, it is to serve the public.

Murphy's Laws
of
Business & Finance for Warriors

Throughout recorded history the role of Professional Warrior has remained the most exalted of professions. Warriors represent the cream of their nation's manhood. They proudly serve and protect the common man, the fabric of society, the ruling authority.

But all warriors know that Father Time is a stealthy killer. He gradually takes his toll. No warrior can sally forth into combat forever, year after year. On the hi-tech battlefield of today, there is scant room for senior-citizen Grunts.

Advanced age induces many warriors to trade in their cammies and combat boots for business suits and wingtips. Then they enter the cutthroat world of Business & Finance, where the enemy smiles and shakes hands before stabbing you in the back. The gung-ho warrior of yesterday often degenerates into a corporate drone. He finds that all the core values in life have changed.

To prepare warriors for this new battlefield, Murphy offers his insight into the back-stabbing world of Business & Finance:

The first myth of management is that it exists.

The second myth of management is that skill will produce success.

The two most vital ingredients of management are (1) indecision and (2) charlatanism.

Business managers are so wrapped up in business *theory* that they can not see the business *reality* of anything.

Most managers manage by the book -- even though they do not know which book.

The managers whose approval is needed the most give it the least.

The degree of technical competence always varies *inversely* with the level of management.

When in doubt, 94 percent of managers will always predict that the current trend will continue.

Sadly, sales ability is usually misinterpreted as managerial ability.

To get any action whatsoever out of management, one must create the illusion of a crisis.

Successful managers theorize that if you can not convince doubters, you must confuse them.

All things considered, corporate life is 9 to 5 against you.

In the corporate world, work is the crabgrass of life.

For every job that exists in the world, there is someone, somewhere, who can not do it. Given enough time and enough promotions, he will eventually arrive at that job, and there he will remain -- habitually bungling the job, frustrating his co-workers, and eroding the efficiency of the organization (thanks, J. Peter).

People are always available for work in the past tense.

No monument has ever been erected to honor a committee.

A committee meeting may be accurately defined as (1) the world's best weapon with which to kill time, (2) an event at which *minutes* are kept and *hours* are lost, and (3) a parasitic life form with eight or more legs and no brain. The most notable characteristics of a committee are listed below:

 - In a committee meeting, the only sure-fire way to get attention is to break wind before speaking.

 - In a committee, pure drivel drives away ordinary drivel.

- In a committee meeting, anyone thinking deep thoughts is thinking about lunch.

- In a committee meeting, the man who smiles has thought of someone to blame.

- In a committee meeting, all attendees exchange information, adjudicate, and compromise. They do not think or create.

- No original thought has *ever* originated in a committee.

- A really new idea affronts any committee.

- To kill any novel idea, assign it to a committee.

- In a Fortune 500 study, the only agreement in 88 percent of all committee meetings was consensus on the next meeting date.

- Committee meetings are a tragic way to waste 1/7 of your life.

- In a committee, a little inaccuracy saves a world of explanation.

- In any committee meeting, creativity varies *inversely* with the number of attendees.

- If a problem prompts many committee meetings, the meetings will become more of a problem than the problem.

- The duration of a committee meeting is *inversely* proportional to the complexity of the problem (if the issue is trivial and everyone understands it, the mindless chatter will last forever).

- Over the past eight years in Fortune 500 companies, 97 percent of all committee reports concluded with the statement: "It is not prudent to change the policy at this time."

- The uselessness of a committee meeting is *directly* proportional to the number of attendees.

- The only thing worse than dreaming you are in a committee meeting, and waking up to find that you *really are* in a committee meeting, is a committee meeting in which you are unable to fall asleep.

- Of the possible committee reactions to a novel idea, the reaction which will occur is the one that will liberate the most hot air.

- In a committee, a motion to adjourn is always in order.

- The six stages of all corporate committee projects:
    1. Great expectations.
    2. Disenchantment.
    3. Mass confusion.
    4. Frantic search for scapegoats.
    5. Punishment of the innocent.
    6. Great distinction for the uninvolved.

- The five committee rules for personal corporate success:
    1. Never arrive on time (only beginners are punctual).
    2. Never say anything until the meeting is almost over (this makes you seem wise).
    3. When speaking, be vague (this prevents irritating others).
    4. When in doubt, propose creation of a sub-committee (this indicates that you have initiative).
    5. Move to adjourn (this makes you popular).

Any bureaucracy which employs 100 or more people is a self-perpetuating empire creating so much internal paperwork that it no longer needs contact with the outside world.

A business bureaucracy is a giant machine operated by drones in which nobody really cares what anyone else is doing.

In any bureaucracy, all real work is done by those who have not yet risen to their level of incompetence.

In any bureaucracy, work seeks the lowest hierarchical level.

In any bureaucracy, expenses or revenues invariably rise to meet the other, no matter which may be in excess.

If a more complicated, costly, and time consuming way of doing something exists, a talented bureaucrat will find it.

The effort expended by any bureaucracy to defend an error is *directly* proportional to the damage caused by the error.

Incompetence increases with the complexity of work performed.

Often, super-competence is more disruptive than incompetence.

Staff needs increase as the level of incompetence increases.

In business, the only reliable way to double your money is to take it out of your wallet and fold it in half.

For business investors, money is not everything. For example, it certainly is not plentiful.

In corporate life, the higher the level, the greater the confusion.

In all corporate endeavors, if it were not for the last minute, nothing would ever get done.

Success in a meeting hinges on the ratio of meeting to eating.

Vacations are productive. When the boss is on one, you get twice as much work done.

Add two weeks to the schedule for unexpected delays, and add two more weeks for unexpected unexpected delays.

All marketing timetable commitments must be multiplied by a factor of 2.5 or more; sales promises by a factor of 0.25 or less.

The firmness of delivery dates is *inversely* proportional to the tightness of the schedule.

Consultants are persons who, when hired to find out what time it is, borrow your watch to find out.

Usually, a consultant is anyone from out of town with a briefcase.

A "subject matter expert" is any person who has lucked out on three or more wild guesses.

A customer should *never* argue with the manufacturer about a production error. The Quality Control checklist *always* will be properly checked off, right down to the holes that are not there.

Skill in manipulating numbers is a talent, not evidence of Divinity.

Infinity is one corporate lawyer waiting on another.

Habitually punctual workers make all of their mistakes on time.

All businesses should live within their incomes, even if they have to borrow to do it.

Corporate profitability is *inversely* proportional to the length and extravagance of the annual Stockholder's Report.

To get a business loan, you must prove that you do not need it.

In business, if you can not be replaced, you can not be promoted.

In business, job security is achieved by spending all of your time doing nothing except lying about the nothing you are doing.

> Murphy's *serious* business advice for all warriors:
> Never forget until too late that the business of life
> is not business, but life.

Murphy's Journey:
Young Warrior to Old Veteran

As teenagers, young Americans of yesteryear grew up with Butch Wax, Green Stamps, roller skate keys, and duck-and-cover drills. They grooved on the music of the Andrews Sisters, The Ink Spots, or The Supremes, and they knew that Ed Sullivan had the best show on the new electronic marvel called television. These budding young adults lived in a visionary and exciting age when the worst thing you usually caught from a woman was a cold.

When their country called, the young patriots made the transition from civilians to American Warriors. They marched off to war in remote and God-forsaken corners of the globe carrying Zippo lighters, P-38s, steel pots, flak jackets, and heat tabs. Amid the perils and misery of combat they lived with malaria, dysentery, ringworm, leeches, and trenchfoot. They were always exhausted, always hungry, always scared of dying, but too afraid and too proud to let it show. They knew that Tony Bennett's heart was somewhere in a mystical sunny place called San Francisco. Many vowed to go there someday and wear flowers in their hair, too, if by some miracle they survived their war.

In battle they carried with them the memory of friends with whom they had shared life in one instant, but who had been shot, mortared, bombed, burned, rocketed, or blasted into oblivion in the next. They carried a nostalgic affection for the world they had left behind, but an intense eternal loyalty to their brothers-in-arms.

These warriors remember places like Pearl Harbor, Iwo Jima, Omaha Beach, and an evil tyrant named Hitler. They stood their ground during the so-called forgotten war in frozen Korea and later during the long Cold War. During the long struggle in Vietnam they ignored the cowardly whiny-babies at home and served their country during her darkest hours since the American Civil War in the previous century. They lived and fought and often died in mud and filth and suffocating heat, or numbing cold, with the rats and the unburied corpses of their friends.

When enemies threatened our nation it was these American Warriors, not the news media, who preserved our freedom of the press. It was these American Warriors, not the church pastors, who preserved our freedom of religion. When foreign despots attacked our country it was these American Warriors, not the lawyers, who preserved our civil liberties. And it was these warriors, not the money-grubbing politicians, who often sacrificed all to guarantee the survival of their homeland.

The warriors who survived came home from their wars and got jobs, raised families, paid taxes, and made society function. As the years roll by, these aging warriors of yesterday find that they have evolved into today's elderly man, an "old fart," an old military veteran, perhaps even a genuine geezer. But to their surprise, they discover that they have gained respectability. Even young people admire them, for society knows they have paid their dues.

To a man, military veterans despise the clamoring media whores and the pitiful apostles of political correctness. They put their faith in their God, their country, and their old brothers-in-arms. They rely on family values, hard work, a good education, and common sense. Freedom is never free. Liberty means responsibilities, and these older military veterans know it.

The aging military veteran of today is the average older man, a neighbor, an uncle, maybe a grandfather. But he is the same man who, in his youth when his country called, gave selflessly of himself and asked for nothing in return. Today's old military veteran is the now-wrinkled warrior of yesterday. He is the man who was willing to sacrifice the flower of his youth so that his countrymen might survive and live in freedom.

Today at sporting events when their National Anthem is played, old military veterans *sing*. They know the words, and they *believe* in them. These old warriors open doors for women, and they do not like the filth and trash on TV. They have moral courage, and the only time they brag is when the conversation turns to their loyal brothers-in-arms or to their children or grandchildren.

For the American Warriors of yesteryear who have evolved into the old military veterans of today, life is good. Old military veterans get *respect*, which in many cases was long overdue. Their country still needs them, their common sense, their work ethic, and their family values -- now, more than ever!

. . . now, a few thoughts from <u>Murphy</u> about growing old . . .

Despite the high cost of living, it remains popular. Most old warriors of yesterday adopt the attitude that they intend to live forever, and so far, so good.

Although growing old is mandatory, growing up is optional. Warriors age, but their definition of Middle Age or Old Age is constant: about ten years older than they are at the moment.

But at some point in life older warriors get *over the hill*. Then to their dismay, they pick up speed. They know that they were born naked, wet, scared, and hungry. Now, year by year it gets worse. Old warriors find that it has been far easier to get old than to get wise. They discover that although time may have been a great healer, it turned out to be a lousy beautician. These warriors have learned to define **Middle Age** as the time when:

- You choose your cereal for the fiber, not the toy.

- You still believe you will feel better in the morning.

- You decide that the best exercise is discretion.

- You are too young for Social Security, but too old for a job.

- You can still do just as much as ever, but would rather not.

- You are at home alone on Friday night, and the phone rings, and you hope that it is not for you.

- You stopped whining about the older generation long ago, and now you whine about the younger one.

- Your broad mind and your narrow waist exchange places.

Warriors of yesteryear never worry too much about **Middle Age** and, unfortunately, they quickly outgrow it. Then they face the yawning abyss of **Old Age**, a terrible price to pay for presumed wisdom. Literally, there is not much future in it (*think* about that one). Old warriors finally know most of life's answers, but no one is asking the questions. They discover that life is like a roll of toilet paper; the closer you get to the end, the faster it goes. They have learned to define **Old Age** as the time in life when:

- You are entering the prime of senility.

- You still could touch your toes -- if they were on your knees.

- Your "wild oats" have matured into prunes and All Bran.

- You are still better than dead -- sort of.

- You can smile, because you know that tomorrow will be worse.

- Your annual cost of the candles exceeds the cost of the cake.

- You approach problems with an open mind and an open fly.

- You have your head together, but your body is falling apart.

- You get absent minded. You get absent minded. You get . .

- You wish "the buck stopped here" (you need the money).

- You find it is easy to meet expenses. They are everywhere.

- You realize it is hard to make a comeback because you have not been anywhere lately.

- You realize that the only time the world beats a path to your door is when you are in the bathroom.

- You spend a lot of time wondering about the "hereafter." You go into the bedroom to get something, and then you wonder what you are hereafter.

- You want to know that if all is not lost, where is it?

- Your steel trap mind has rusted shut.

- Your clear conscience is the result of your faulty memory.

- You plan to be spontaneous and carefree -- tomorrow.

- You remember the carefree days of your youth when you had long hair. Now, you long *for* hair.

- You remember when passing the *driving test* was a big deal in life. Now, passing the *vision test* is a big deal in life.

- You remember the bittersweet days of your youth when *acid rock* was important. Now, *acid reflux* is important.

- You remember the days of your youth when you loved the *Rolling Stones*. Now, you hate your *kidney stones*.

- You remember the bygone days of your youth when all of your friends wanted to move to California because it was *cool*. Now, they want to move to California because it is *warm*.

- You remember when you thought about growing *pot*. Now, like it or not, you are growing a *pot belly*.

- You remember when your *lifetime ambition* was to have a BMW. Now, your *daytime ambition* is to have a BM.

- You remember the *fun* of going to a new "hip" joint. Now, you experience the *agony* of surgery for your new hip joint.

It can no longer be denied. **Old Age** has irrevocably set in. The carefree young warrior of yesterday finds that he has evolved into an ignominious icon of today, a gen-u-ine **Geezer**.

Being a geezer has some drawbacks. You often have to change your underwear after each sneeze. And if a good-looking sultry woman pleads with you, "Let's go upstairs and make love," you are forced to reply:

"Pick *one*, I can't do both!"

Yet, there are plenty of perks for geezers. Life is not totally the pits. Your supply of brain cells is finally down to a manageable level, and your eyes can not possibly get much worse. You enjoy hearing about your friends' operations, and your only heated arguments are about Social Security. A ringing telephone never bothers you after 8:00 pm because nobody you know is awake then, either. In many ways Geezers are lucky, for they know that:

- There is nothing left to learn the hard way.

- You *can* live without sex (but not without glasses).

- Things you buy now will never wear out.

- Your investment in health insurance is beginning to pay off.

- Kidnappers are no longer interested in you.

- In a mass hostage situation, you will be released first.

- There is no longer *any* reason to try to hold your stomach in.

- Women: going bra-less pulls the wrinkles out of your face.

- Your joints are better meteorologists than the TV weatherman.

- You no longer care where your spouse goes.

- "Getting a little action" means you do not need more fiber.

- "Getting lucky" means you found your car at the mall.

- You are told to slow down by the doctor, not the police.

From now on your secrets are absolutely, positively, safe with all of your friends, because they can not remember them, either.

Murphy's Writing Rules
for the
Modern Warrior

In the medieval past, warriors were men of action, men of few words. They charged headlong into the fray, killed the enemy and his evil cohorts, and then went home. No verbal expertise was required. Warriors let their lethal skills do the talking.

As the centuries rolled past, verbal communication gradually became necessary in warfare. Still later, written messages came into vogue. Warriors initially tried to keep their correspondence simple. When the Roman Legions of Julius Caesar vanquished the bad guys at Zela in 47 BC, Caesar's written dispatch to the Roman Senate contained just six words: "I came, I saw, I conquered."

Sadly, the life of professional warriors grew more complicated and sophisticated over the years. Today most hi-tech weapons systems require huge technical manuals. A coordinated attack is set in motion not with a verbal command -- such as, *Charge!* -- but with a gargantuan Operational Order consisting of hundreds of pages of written details. In a barracks environment, today's warrior must wade through a tremendous pile of written instructions about an ever-increasing host of responsibilities and functions.

In addition to their fighting expertise, warriors of today must hone their literary skills. Professional warriors must become accomplished *writers*. They must adhere to accepted, although confusing, principles of grammar and composition. Warriors must rely on Simon & Schuster's *Handbook for Writers*, a dictionary and thesaurus, and a computer. Above all else, the wise warrior of today never ignores Murphy's Writing Rules:

To avoid looking ignorant, do not use no double negatives.

Warriors, remember that verbs has to agree with their subject.

Use capital letters for places like new york, atlanta, and dallas.

Badd speling will detract from an otherwize exsellant repport.

Each pronoun should agree with their antecedent.

Just between you and I, case is important.

Beware of sinister irregular verbs which has cropped up.

A good writer must not shift your point of view.

If you must resort to dangling, never use participles.

Write good, join clauses good like a conjunction should.

And *never* use conjunctions to start your sentences.

Do not ever use a run-on sentence you have to punctuate it.

A few thoughts about sentence fragments.

In letters themes reports articles and stuff like that Murphy suggests using commas to keep strings of words separated.

But, do not ever, use commas, which are not, necessary.

Remember, guy's, it is important to use apostrophe's right.

Do not abbrev. in formal correspondence.

Proof your writing. Check to see if you any words out.

In Murphy's personal opinion he thinks that the author when he is writing should not get into the daily bad habit of making use of too many needless and unnecessary and extra words which he does not really need to use in his written correspondence to other people.

Never, never, never use a preposition to end a sentence with.

-- Last but not least, avoid cliches like the plague. --

Murphy's Guide:
The Chinese Zodiac
for
Warriors

Warriors, are you frustrated by life? Unhappy with your moon sign (Aquarius, Pisces, Scorpio, or whatever)? Unlucky in love? Financial problems? Do you often strike out in the game of sex and seduction? Under a voodoo hex? Has fate stacked the deck of life against you? Does there seem to be no way out?

Do not despair! Murphy suggests that you turn to the Chinese Zodiac. Those who heed the principles of the ancient Chinese have found the secrets of happiness, wealth, and amorous bliss.

Time after time, science has proved that Astrology is bunk! Conversely, the Chinese Zodiac "signs" are based on the true cyclical nature of time (as opposed to the erroneous *linear* concept which is popular in the Western World). The planets orbit the sun in a predictable cycle. The Chinese calendar incorporates this infallible 12 year cosmic pattern. Your knowledge of this cycle is the key to all happiness and success in life.

Many centuries ago Chinese soothsayers discovered that the *day* of a warrior's birth does not dictate his destiny. What matters is the *year* in which he was born, because time and history inevitably repeat themselves. As scientific studies have recently confirmed, the traits with which a person is born today will be duplicated in people who are born 12 years later.

Twenty-six centuries ago Buddha (c 563-483 BC) bestowed an animal "sign" upon each of the 12 years in the cosmic cycle. Each of these signs represents one year in the Chinese Zodiac.

Murphy has consolidated these invaluable gems of wisdom for the benefit of professional warriors. Look below and find the year of your birth. Then read your Chinese Zodiac "sign" and unlock the timeless cosmic secrets which dictate human nature:

-- The 12 Signs of the Chinese Zodiac --

Year of the Rat (for people born in 1912, 1924, 1936, 1948, 1960, 1972, 1984, 1996, 2008, or 2020):

People born in the Year of the Rat are noted for their personal charm, generosity, imagination, and their inclination toward opportunism. They enjoy the company of other people and love to socialize or work in groups. They strive hard to achieve their goals and obtain possessions, and they are noted for their thriftiness with money. Their ambitions are boundless, and they usually are able to accumulate vast material possessions.

On the other hand, Rat people are absolute perfectionists. When events do not go their way, they often fly into quick-tempered fits of rage or frustration. This, tragically, limits their ability to work effectively with others. Also, to their detriment they are prone to vicious gossip. They are invariably overly critical of others, causing their interpersonal relationships to suffer.

Soulmates: When inclined toward passionate affairs of the heart, Rat people are most compatible with members of the opposite sex who were born in the year of the Monkey or Ox.

Disaster: To avoid misery, a Rat must avoid Horse people.

Year of the Ox (for people born in 1913, 1925, 1937, 1949, 1961, 1973, 1985, 1997, 2009, or 2021):

People born in the Year of the Ox are talented, smart, articulate, and virtuous. Although they speak seldom and softly, they speak with great eloquence. Through their intuitive personal conduct, they inspire trust and confidence in others. High inner work standards enable them to succeed in business and interpersonal affairs. Ox people are deep-thinking philosophers, and they relish the company of like-minded intelligent friends. They are inevitably the most dependable member of their social circle.

Unfortunately, however, Ox people are inclined toward a host of unreasonable fears. And despite their easy-going reticent nature, they are rarely able to conceal their great weakness: a fierce temper, spurred on by a never-back-down stubborn streak. They hate to fail, and they despise being opposed. Their inner battle against anger and conflict saps much of their strength.

Soulmates: When the melodious strings of their hearts have been

strummed, Ox people are most compatible with members of the opposite sex who were born in the year of the Rooster or Rat.
Disaster: To skirt disaster, an Ox must never consort with Goats.

Year of the Tiger (for people born in 1914, 1926, 1938, 1950, 1962, 1974, 1986, 1998, 2010, or 2022):
Tiger people are sensitive, given to deep thinking, and capable of extreme sympathy. Others have great respect for them, for they are courageous and powerful. They fear neither authority nor foes, and they go boldly into the breach in situations wherein lesser persons quake in fear and inactivity. Others are drawn to Tigers because of their obvious courage and audacity.

Conversely, their strengths are a double-edged sword. Tiger people are suspicious of others, and this suspicion often degenerates into cynicism and paranoia. This inevitably causes conflict with those in positions of authority. Also, people born in the year of the Tiger generally make snap decisions without the benefit of all the facts and circumstances. This usually results in poor choices.

Soulmates: When their hearts seek intimate company, Tiger people are most compatible with members of the opposite sex who were born in the year of the Horse, Dragon, or Dog.
Disaster: Tigers must steer clear of Monkeys at all costs.

Year of the Rabbit (for people born in 1915, 1927, 1939, 1951, 1963, 1975, 1987, 1999, 2011, or 2023):
Rabbit people are intuitive, talented, and ambitious. They are also virtuous, reserved, and endowed with refined tastes. They are admired and trusted. Although fond of gossip, they are tactful and generally kind. Rabbit people seldom lose their temper. They are deceptively clever at business matters and, being conscientious, never back out of an agreement.

Yet, Rabbits are obsessed with gambling, and unfortunately they seem to be cursed with perpetual bad luck. They have an uncanny knack for always choosing the wrong thing, or the right thing at the wrong time. This leads to financial disaster, which explains why so many Rabbits have to rely on the generosity of their friends.

Soulmates: When their hearts yearn for amorous companionship, Rabbit people are most compatible with members of the opposite sex who were born in the year of the Goat or Pig.

<u>Disaster</u>: To avoid doom, Rabbits must shun Roosters.

Year of the Dragon (for people born in 1916, 1928, 1940, 1952, 1964, 1976, 1988, 2000, 2012, or 2024):

Dragons are healthy, energetic, excitable, short-tempered, and stubborn. They also are honest, sensitive, brave, and they inspire confidence and trust. In many ways Dragon people are the most eccentric of any in the eastern zodiac. They make no flowery speeches and they never brag, but invariably they are full of enthusiasm and vitality. They are popular among their peers because of their inspirational nature.

Nonetheless, Dragon people inevitably turn out to be far too softhearted. Tragically, this trait gives unscrupulous persons the opportunity to take advantage of them. Dragons try desperately to conceal this weakness, usually to no avail.

<u>Soulmates</u>: When the thick fog of romance hangs in the air, Dragon people are most compatible with members of the opposite sex who were born in the year of the Snake, Tiger, or Monkey.

<u>Disaster</u>: Dragons must never keep company with Dogs.

Year of the Snake (for people born in 1917, 1929, 1941, 1953, 1965, 1977, 1989, 2001, 2013, or 2025):

People born in the Year of the Snake seem calm and carefree on the surface, but they are secretly intense and passionate in private. Because they are stingy, Snakes rarely have to worry about money. Although they are considered to be wise, they reject conventional achievements. Instead, they favor ideas, concepts and theories. Snake people are analytical, obsessive, and goal oriented. They measure their life in terms of tangible accomplishment and friendships. Yet, Snakes tend to rely on themselves, preferring not to trust the judgement of others.

Unfortunately these traits often transform a Snake into a social loner or a recluse. Cursed with their eccentric nature, Snakes often fail to get needed advice or help from others. Further, because they tend to be perfectionists, they easily become frustrated when things do not go their way in life.

<u>Soulmates</u>: When their heartstrings search for a melody, Snakes are most compatible with members of the opposite sex who were born in the year of the Dragon or Rooster.

Disaster: To circumvent calamity, Snakes must avoid Pigs.

Year of the Horse (for people born in 1918, 1930, 1942, 1954, 1966, 1978, 1990, 2002, 2014, or 2026):

People born in the Year of the Horse are popular. They are cheerful, skillful with money, wise, and perceptive. They are impatient and tenacious about everything in life, especially their daily work, and their capacity for material achievement is astounding. Gregarious and outgoing, they seek entertainment and find pleasure when in large crowds.

However, Horses inevitably talk too much, and this has an adverse effect on potential friendships. In addition, they rarely listen to advice. Worse yet, they have a pronounced weakness for insincere overtures by members of the opposite sex, and this tends to result in folly and a life of misery.

Soulmates: When their hearts and souls pine for amorous activity, Horse people are most compatible with members of the opposite sex who are a Tiger, Goat, or Dog.

Disaster: To thwart failure, Horses must shy away from Rats.

Year of the Goat (for people born in 1919, 1931, 1943, 1955, 1967, 1979, 1991, 2003, 2015, or 2027):

Goat people are elegant and highly accomplished in the arts. They seem to be, at first glance, better off than those born in the zodiac's other cycles. They are secretly religious, but they try to hide it behind a devil-may-care facade. Always overly vocal in speech, they are intensely passionate about what they do and what they believe in. Goat people strive for achievement and for the best things in life. They enjoy the material things that money can bring, and they spend lavishly.

Sadly, although Goat people spend *lavishly*, they spend *foolishly*. This weakness leaves them with financial problems that will plague them for life. Therefore, they are often pessimistic and frustrated about their lot. They pine for the better things that money can bring and the causes in which they believe. Tragically, their dreams usually exceed their financial means.

Soulmates: Goat people, in their amorous endeavors, are most compatible with members of the opposite sex who were born in the year of the Rabbit, Pig, or Horse.

Disaster: To stave off doom, Goats must never befriend an Ox.

Year of the Monkey (for people born in 1920, 1932, 1944, 1956, 1968, 1980, 1992, 2004, 2016, or 2028):
Monkeys are the erratic animals of the 12 year planetary cycle. Clever, skillful, and flexible, they are remarkably inventive and original and can solve the most difficult problems with ease. They have the ability to be successful in any field. They have knowledge, wisdom, excellent memories, and a strong desire to succeed. In addition, their cheerful personality is a great asset in interpersonal relationships.

Nonetheless, Monkeys always want to do things *now*. If they can not start immediately, they become discouraged and often abandon worthy projects in anger. Although effective in making decisions, they often look down on others. Their unwarranted anger and their vacillating nature thwart many of their goals in life.

Soulmates: In matters of lust and love, Monkey people are most compatible with members of the opposite sex who are a Dragon or a Rat.

Disaster: A wise Monkey will never dally with a Tiger.

Year of the Rooster (for people born in 1921, 1933, 1945, 1957, 1969, 1981, 1993, 2005, 2017, or 2029):
People born in the year of the Rooster are deep thinkers, capable, and talented. They like to be busy and are dedicated to work. Fortunately for society they dare to dream of possibilities beyond the scope of the average mind. At times they may "build castles in the air," but many of their visions for the future bear fortuitous fruit for all mankind.

Yet, Roosters are eccentric. They usually have rather difficult relationships with others because of their irritating habit of insisting that they get their own way. Although Roosters give the outward impression that they are adventurous, they secretly are inwardly timid. Their emotions, like their fortunes, swing from very high to very low. They live their lives trying to prove to the world that they are superior to others, and true happiness usually is elusive.

Soulmates: In matters of the heart, Rooster people are most compatible with members of the opposite sex who were born in the year of the Ox or the Snake.

<u>Disaster</u>: For a happy life, Roosters must avoid Rabbits.

Year of the Dog (for people born in 1922, 1934, 1946, 1958, 1970, 1982, 1994, 2006, 2018, or 2030):

Dog people possess many of the most desirable traits of human nature. They have a refined sense of loyalty and honesty. Like their real-world namesake, a Dog person will never betray a friend. Further, they inspire confidence in others because they know how to keep secrets. They care little for wealth, yet somehow always seem to have lots of money. Most of all, they are valued for their faithfulness and honesty.

Conversely, Dog people are selfish, stubborn, and eccentric. At social events they frequently seem emotionally cold and distant. They find fault with many things and are noted for their sharp tongues. Cynicism, sarcasm, defensiveness, and pessimism are the most readily recognizable faults of a Dog person.

<u>Soulmates</u>: When the winds of passion fan the flame of ardor, Dog people are most compatible with members of the opposite sex who were born in the year of the Horse, Tiger, or Rabbit.

<u>Disaster</u>: To succeed in life, a Dog must keep Dragons at bay.

Year of the Pig (for people born in 1923, 1935, 1947, 1959, 1971, 1983, 1995, 2007, 2019, or 2031):

Those born in the Year of the Pig are chivalrous and gallant. Whatever they do, they do with all their strength. For Pigs there is no left or right, and there is no retreat. In life, Pigs charge straight ahead, attacking all obstacles without delay or debate. When they create a friendship, it is for life. They prize loyalty above all else. They have an unquenchable thirst for knowledge, and they study and become well informed.

However, all Pigs are quick tempered. Although they hate arguments and quarreling, they are inevitably drawn into conflicts with others. No matter how minor a problem seems to be, they somehow find a way to argue and make it worse. Further, their impulsive nature alienates those involved in joint endeavors.

<u>Soulmates</u>: When the bud of romance has burst into bloom, Pig people are most compatible with members of the opposite sex who were born in the year of the Rabbit or Goat.

<u>Disaster</u>: To avoid peril, a wise Pig never consorts with a Snake.

Murphy's Review
for Warriors:
History of Stupidity

An historical review is needed. Government institutionalized *stupidity* in the Thirteenth Century in Medieval Europe. When a King was having a bad day, he often took out his wrath or frustration on his staff, his Royal Court. Consequently, to protect their necks from the executioner's ax, the Royal Court came up with a self-defense strategy. They began the custom of bringing in a local idiot or *retard* to make the King laugh. Over time these local idiots became known as Court Jesters.

Contrary to present-day belief, Court Jesters were not bright or witty, and they enjoyed no elevated social status. Conversely, they were chosen for their *sheer stupidity*. Many were so retarded that they lacked the power of speech, and by today's standards they would have been categorized as certified imbeciles. The Royal Court delighted in subjecting these unfortunate souls to all manner of indignity and torture, the "fun and games" of the day.

Today's image of a Court Jester usually brings to mind a clown attired in checkered tights and wearing a motley hat adorned with bells. That image has some basis in fact. But the checkered tights were actually scraps of colored cloth that the homeless buffoon had pulled around himself to keep warm in winter. The bells were attached to his hat by the Royal Court, thinking that the tinkling would further befuddle the poor man and amuse the King.

In any event, each Court Jester historically had an unhappy and short life. The King usually tired of watching the same idiot after a day or two. Records show that the King then decreed that the man be beheaded to put him out of his misery and to rid society of the burden of supporting him. Then the Royal Court would drag in a new Court Jester to amuse the King.

Like death and taxes, stupidity has remained with us over the centuries. Today we know that stupidity is not a sin; stupid people can not help being stupid. But stupidity can not be cured with money, or through education, or by legislation. In the game of life, stupidity is a Capital Offense. The sentence is death, there is no mercy or appeal, and the execution is carried out without pity.

American Warriors, look out! Stupidity has gained a foothold in the world of military science and technology. When stupid people input their stupid ideas into a military computer, nothing except their stupid ideas will come out. But this fancy new computer-enhanced stupidity, emanating from an expensive and complex machine, is somehow ennobled. Often no one has the courage to criticize it. Therefore, warriors should be forewarned:

Stupidity is the hobgoblin of ignorant little minds.

Stupidity is the world's greatest armor against reason and logic.

Never underestimate the power of human stupidity.

Never underestimate the power of stupid people in large groups.

Artificial computer intelligence is no match for genetic stupidity.

Stupidity is the most powerful force in the universe.

Stupidity knows no boundaries of time and place.

One can be sincere and well intentioned, and still be stupid.

For those who are afflicted, stupidity is bliss.

You are only young once, but the afflicted are stupid forever.

Stupidity cramps any conversation.

A little stupidity can go a long way.

Stupidity is no excuse. It is the *real thing*.

Stupidity plus more stupidity equals gross stupidity.

Gross stupidity is far worse than run-of-the-mill stupidity.

Stupidity is not only more deplorable than we imagine, it is more deplorable than we *can* imagine.

New theories flourish in direct proportion to their stupidity.

Most stupid people can now and then spot wrong answers, but they never spot wrong questions.

For stupid people, mistakes are too much fun to make only once.

Stupid people never make the same mistake twice. They make it three, four, five, or six times.

Stupidity, combined with good intentions, is the most disastrous combination on Earth.

Only a stupid person is always at his best.

"Continuing education" may be expensive, but it is not nearly as expensive as continuing stupidity.

Stupidity is the sad mentality that induces one to keep throwing steaks to a tiger, hoping that the tiger will become a vegetarian.

True, a little knowledge may be a dangerous thing, but a little stupidity is far, far worse.

Most of being wise is knowing what you are stupid about, for everyone is stupid -- about something.

But, stupid people do not know what they do not know.

Forgetfulness among liars equates to stupidity (if you are going to lie consistently and successfully, you will need a good memory).

If five million people say a stupid thing, it is still a stupid thing.

When "stupidity" is a sufficient explanation, resist the temptation to resort to any other.

Most of what is attributed to malice actually should be attributed to sheer stupidity.

The probability of someone watching you is *directly* proportional to the degree of stupidity of your conduct.

Usually, stupid is as stupid does.

On the other hand, if it is stupid, yet works, it is not stupid.

When a delicate component needs repair, stupid people never force it. They just use a bigger hammer.

Stupid people drink downstream from the herd.

When stupid people find themselves in a hole, they keep digging.

When constipated, only a stupid person will take three sleeping pills and three doses of a laxative on the same night -- and smile.

Only a stupid person would try to hold a cat and operate a Dust Buster at the same time.

Only stupid people try to train dogs to guard their hamburgers.

From time to time, stupid people try to improve their lot in life by reading. They should be commended for their attempt to better their lives. Yet, Murphy has found that these efforts rarely bear fruit. According to library research records, the type of book most often selected by stupid people requires crayons. In more advanced instances, pencils are needed to connect the dots.

Other stupid people try to select publications which one actually can *read*. Using library publication selection data from Europe and America, and incorporating computerized search methods, Murphy has compiled a list of the most popular such books. A dozen of these books fall into the ***military/political*** category. Murphy noted that there is a common thread running through each military book on this list. Each of these 12 books is <u>extremely brief</u>. Murphy lists them in descending order of popularity:

1. Fighter Aces of the Iraqi Air Force
2. Morality, Ethics, and the Clinton Presidency
3. Brain Teasers for Marines
4. Carrier Landings and the B-2
5. Rappelling for Sailors
6. Diplomacy and Courtesy: The Life and Philosophy of Gen. George S. Patton Jr.
7. Gourmet Recipes for MREs
8. Golf Courses of Vietnam
9. Under Fire with a Combat Photographer: The War Memoirs of Albert Gore Jr.
10. Victory the McNamara Way
11. Airborne Assaults of the Viet Cong
12. Hitler, Mussolini, and the 1000 Year Alliance

Light travels faster than sound. That explains why most stupid people look normal *until* you hear them speak.

Murphy's Warning for Warriors: Adages for Fools

Fools are the unfortunate souls who putter through life with their mouths open and their minds shut. Neither medicine nor therapy can blunt the tragic symptoms, and there is no known cure. The affliction is a life-long curse.

A *fool* and a *stupid* person are not the same thing. A stupid person has been intellectually shortchanged at birth. On the other hand, a fool may be smart, and both his mind and his mouth may function -- but not at the same time.

Because of the damage they can do in the world, fools have a special day of recognition, *April Fools' Day*. Until the Sixteenth Century the world celebrated the beginning of each new year on the first day of April. But in 1582, Pope Gregory XIII (1502-1585) scrapped the Julian calendar and introduced his new Gregorian calendar to the Christian world. According to the new calendar, each new year begins on the first day of January. The monarchs of Europe eventually adopted the Gregorian calendar, and citizens began celebrating each new year on the first day of January.

Observers of the new year festivities soon spotted a glitch. The *proverbial ten percent* of the population "did not get the word" or refused to adapt to change. These *slow-learners* continued to assume that the new year began on the first day of April. Refusing to bow to convention, they continued to celebrate the first day of April with revelry and dancing, three months after the rest of the civilized world. Society soon came up with a descriptive moniker for the nonconformists, "the April fools." And because "the April fools" celebrated the new year on the first day of April, that day gradually became the *April Fools' Day*.

April Fools' Day is now the day to recognize all fools, those who are mentally out-of-step with society. According to convention, this is the day to play harmless pranks, the day to dupe some fool into accepting some premise that is obviously false.

Yet, warriors must be wary of fools. With their minds and

mouths irrevocably out of sync, there is no limit to the damage and misery they can initiate in society. Murphy forewarns warriors that the following adages apply worldwide to all fools:

It is humanly impossible to make a weapons system foolproof, because fools are deceptively ingenious.

Historically, so-called "foolproof systems" never take into account the inherent ingenuity of fools.

Ingenious fools can break anything, up to and including anvils.

Nothing is foolproof to a talented fool.

To a fool, delusions are functional.

Fools often get lost in thought, for it is unfamiliar territory.

Fools laugh last, but only because they think the slowest.

The problem with fools and their gene pool: no lifeguard.

Fools rush in where fools usually rush in.

There is no fool like an old fool -- you can not beat experience.

Fools consistently *pass up* excellent opportunities to *shut up*.

Fools rarely resist good opportunities to say nothing.

Only a potential fool will argue with a known fool.

If a run-of-the-mill fool argues with a complete fool, bystanders can never determine who is who.

A complete fool causes more damage than a run-of-the-mill fool.

Run-of-the-mill fools kick cow chips. Complete fools kick cow chips on a hot day.

If a run-of-the-mill fool argues with a complete fool, he must do so on the mental level of the complete fool.

Only a fool will wrestle with pigs and argue with idiots.

Only a complete fool will slap a man who is chewing tobacco.

A hungry fool will eat *several* boxes of prunes -- and smile.

Most fools deserve each other.

If there are nine fools in the ring, a wise warrior could jump into their midst and start reciting Shakespeare. Yet, to onlookers the wise warrior merely would be the tenth fool.

Those tempted to rave at fools run the risk of becoming one.

Controversy tends to equalize fools and wise men. Unfortunately, this is a fool's one great advantage.

Wise men learn more from fools than fools learn from wise men.

Wise men learn from the mistakes of other people, but fools insist on making their own mistakes.

A wise warrior learns by reading, or observing, or listening. Fools learn by peeing on the electric fence for themselves.

Smoking a pipe gives a wise man time to think, and a fool just something to grit his teeth on.

A fool always wants to be right, for he knows that he is incapable of changing his mind.

Only the fools and the dead are not open to suggestion.

Cynicism is a fool's substitute for intelligence.

An argument between fools is an exchange of ignorance.

All men may be fools for up to five minutes each day. Wise men have learned not to exceed the limit.

To err, now and then, is human. But fools consistently run out of eraser before running out of pencil.

A fool may be accurately described as a person who goes through life with his mouth open and his mind closed.

Often, it is ethically wrong to allow fools to keep their money.

One way or another, a fool and his money are soon parted.

A fool's version of reason is called prejudice.

Only fools try to stop the march of time.

Fools chatter and chatter when they have nothing to say.

Fools would chatter less if they stopped and listened to themselves.

If you do not say a foolish thing, no one can truthfully quote you. Fools have yet to figure this out.

A talented fool will usually avoid the small errors while sweeping on to his grand fallacy.

All kookies are not found in a jar.

Only fools argue with institutions that buy ink by the barrel.

If there is a wrong thing to say, a fool will inevitably say it.

A drunken fool's words are his sober thoughts.

By chance, even fools are right now and then. Unfortunately they *think* they are right all of the time.

Fools start out with absolutely nothing, and they still have it.

In the ongoing battle between fools and the world, the odds definitely favor the world.

A fool will fling himself from the room, fling himself upon his horse, and madly ride off in all directions.

Only a fool would give his right arm to be ambidextrous.

To a fool, two wrongs are only the beginning.

When things look desperate and there seems to be no way out, there is usually one person who is willing to step forward and take charge. Unfortunately that person is usually a fool.

A fool is the person who, immediately before his untimely demise, shouted to his friends, "Hey, guys, watch this!"

It takes a boy almost two decades to become a man. But if he also is a fool, it shows in two minutes.

Wise men simplify the complex; fools complicate the simple.

One of the great tragedies of life is that fools always have louder voices than wise men.

Never approach a horse from the rear, a goat from the front, or a fool from any direction.

However big the fool, there usually is a bigger one to admire him.

Warriors, beware, for there are well dressed foolish ideas, just as there are well dressed fools.

Murphy's Rules
for
Dating a Warrior's Daughter

Teenage boys! When you see the father of the girl you wish to date, do your homework. Is he a warrior? A military veteran? If so, Murphy knows the rules for your survival.

You may think the father is a balding, dim-witted, middle-aged reprobate. Although that is likely true, do not be deceived. Old warriors and military veterans have *been there* and *done that*. When it comes to sex and seduction, they know every sneaky little trick in your book, plus a hundred more devious tricks you are not smart enough to comprehend.

If you expect to stay alive while sniffing around at a warrior's home, memorize and heed Murphy's Rules. To make it easy for you to comply with them, Murphy has written these 17 rules from the warrior's point of view. In effect, "the warrior" is giving you this excellent advice. Ignore these rules at your own peril:

Rule 1: If your vehicle stops in my driveway and you honk the horn, I shall assume you are announcing your desire to deliver a gift. You definitely will not be picking anything up.

Rule 2: Exit your vehicle and speak the password. Turn, face your vehicle, and place both hands on the top. After I have searched you, interrogated you, and checked a minimum of two forms of photo-identification, I *may* allow you to stand at ease by the steps to my front porch.

Rule 3: However, if I tell you to stand by your car, stay there. You may stand at ease, but do not wander off. My attack dogs are always on the lookout for fresh meat.

Rule 4: If you wait and more than an hour passes, do not shuffle your feet or fidget. My daughter likely is still putting on her makeup, a process which may take several more hours. If you wish to pass the time by doing something useful, raise your hand, speak, and request permission to wash my truck.

Rule 5: Do not be tempted to try to get to know me by mindlessly jabbering about sports, politics, cars, or similar childish foolishness. Unless I tell you to speak, keep your mouth shut.

Rule 6: Be very afraid. In my presence, keep your hands out of your pockets. If you jingle your loose coins or rattle your car keys, I may mistake it for the sound of bad guys in the wire when my PTSD starts acting up.

Rule 7: Never lie to me. During any random interrogation to which I may subject you, never lie. When it comes to my little girl, I am your terminal nightmare, the all-knowing and merciless Deity of your universe. You will have one chance to tell me the truth, the whole truth, and nothing but the truth. I have (1) no scruples, (2) a closet full of automatic weapons, (3) a footlocker full of ammo, (4) a back-hoe, and (5) forty-six wooded acres behind the house. Do not tempt me.

Rule 8: I trust that you are a popular young fellow with many opportunities to socialize with other girls. However, once you have dated my daughter, you will date no other girl until my daughter is absolutely finished with you.

Rule 9: When and if my daughter is finally ready, the two of you are free to go. However, first I will ask you what time you will deliver my daughter back to my home. The only words you are authorized to speak are: "Whenever you say, Sir!"

Rule 10: You must *never* take my daughter to:
- Places where there are no nuns or policemen within sight.
- Places where there is darkness.
- Places where there are beds, sofas, recliners, and such.
- Places where there is music or dancing.
- Places where there is happiness or holding hands.

- Places where the temperature is warm enough to induce my daughter to wear shorts, a tank top, a bathing suit, or anything other than insulated coveralls and a hooded sweater.

Rule 11: *If* my daughter agrees, you may take her to:
- Nursing homes, churches, government offices, and hospitals.
- Military parades and patriotic functions (during the daytime).
- Outdoor athletic or auto racing events (during the daytime).
- Movies (during the daytime) *if* there are no romantic themes, and *if* you and my daughter do not sit in adjacent seats. Note: movies which feature chain saws, auto racing, wrestling, or hand-to-hand combat are preferred.

Rule 12: You may look at my daughter *if* she consents and *if* you do not look at anything below her neck.

Rule 13: You may never touch my daughter in any manner or under any circumstances. If I ever discover your hands on my daughter, I *will* remove them. It *will* be painful.

Rule 14: If you ever make my daughter cry, I will make you cry a lot more before I kill you.

Rule 15: In this enlightened age, I trust you know that sexual conduct without using "protection" can kill you. Make no mistake. If you even *daydream* about sexual conduct with my daughter, I *am* the protection, and I *will* kill you.

Rule 16: While you are away from my home with my little girl, the voices in my head always tell me to clean and reload my weapons. While I wait for you to return, I do what the voices tell me to do. *Think* about it.

Rule 17: When you return to my driveway with my little girl, keep both hands (1) in sight and (2) on the wheel. Do not even *consider* exiting your vehicle. Shout in a loud voice that you have brought my daughter back home. Once she has safely entered my front door, drive away immediately. The camouflaged face you may see in the window is mine.

Murphy's Computer Laws for Warriors

In the prehistoric era, warriors "computed" on their fingers. If a warrior spied *three bad guys* sneaking toward his cave, he would hold up *three fingers* to alert and inform his brothers-in-arms. This simple system worked well unless the number of bad guys exceeded a warrior's number of fingers.

As the centuries rolled past, "math" for combat got a lot more complex. Warriors had to learn to communicate numerically in writing. As warfare evolved, combat engineers designed medieval **weapons of mass destruction**: huge siege engines, catapults, rams, and the fortified rolling towers of the day. The feared trebuchet could hurl a 300 pound stone over 600 feet to batter down enemy castle walls. Military builders had to perform complex numerical calculations during construction of these weapons.

Earlier, mathematical whizzes had developed the first digital computer, the abacus. With beads strung on two wires, five on top and two on the bottom, the abacus proved to be a great aid for engineers and warriors alike. Hundreds of years later in England, William Oughtred invented the slide rule in 1632, allowing more complex computations to be performed.

William Thompson, an English scientist, developed a written description of a basic analog computer in 1876. Of course, the technology of the day prevented anyone from actually building one. But in 1930 at the Massachusetts Institute of Technology, Vannevar Bush used the written specifications of Thompson and built what he called the "Automatic Analyzer," the world's first functional *analog* computer. This type of computer became the brain of automated fire control weapons systems.

Seven years later at Harvard University, Howard Aiken combined 78 mechanical adding machines with hundreds of electrical relays. He controlled this monstrosity with perforated player-piano type paper tape. Presto! He created a *digital* computer, the "Automatic Sequence Controlled Calculator," which the U.S. Army used for complex mathematical calculations during World War II.

The "Electronic Numerical Integrator and Computer" was born after the war. Using over 18,000 new vacuum tubes instead of the old mechanical relays, the new computer could do 5000 additions per second. Military computers were here to stay!

Today the vacuum tubes, relays, and printed circuits have gone the way of the dinosaur. New technology has replaced them with microchips. Computers have gotten smaller and smaller, faster and faster. They permeate all aspects of modern military life. Warriors who have a desk likely have a computer sitting on it, and all warriors have computers built into their smart weapons.

True, computers may be inherently evil, but they have become a *necessary evil* for the modern combatant. Murphy warns all warriors to beware of the "garbage in, garbage out" syndrome. Also, the successful warrior of today should be forewarned:

No warrior ever *really* learns to curse until he uses a computer.

The only language common to all programmers is profanity.

If builders built houses the way programmers write programs, the first woodpecker to come along would destroy civilization.

If you force computer programmers to write programs in simple English, you will discover that programmers *do not know how* to write in simple English.

Hint for warriors: never program and drink beer at the same time.

To err is human, but to *really* foul things up requires a computer.

Computers can solve all sorts of problems, except those things in this world that just do not add up.

Any system which relies on computer reliability is unreliable.

In today's commercial marketplace, the only merchants guaranteed to make money are those who sell computer paper.

In any computer program, any bug that can creep in will creep in.

All military computer programs contain five or more bugs.

And, hidden somewhere, there is *always* one more bug.

Bug-free software is never.

If a program works, it must be changed. If a program does not work, it must be saved and backed up.

Any given program, when running, is obsolete.

The faster a computer is, the sooner it will crash.

All new computer systems generate all new computer problems.

A computer can make as many mistakes and cause as much damage in two nanoseconds as 2000 men who toil for 2000 years.

Modern logic: if it is not in the computer, it does not exist.

If a computer cable and a connector are picked at random, the probability that they are compatible is equal to zero.

The probability of a peripheral being compatible with a given computer is *inversely* proportional to the need for that peripheral.

The likelihood that an untested floppy diskette will have bad sectors is *directly* proportional to the significance of the data stored on that untested diskette.

After a floppy diskette has been dropped, the likelihood that it will be stepped upon is *directly* proportional to its value.

When transmitting data, all noise bursts will occur so as to cause the most serious errors in data transmission, regardless of the amount of noise present.

The chance of software being neurotic (for the uneducated, that means it develops *bugs*) is *directly* proportional to the amount of confusion the neurosis will cause.

If there are *n* bytes in a crucial software program, the available storage space will be *n-1* bytes.

If two programs are chosen at random, they will be incompatible.

When two people share a computer, their software preferences will differ in every possible way.

Computer experts never die, they just lose their memory.

Military consumer expectations will always outpace advances in military software technology.

A warrior who laughs last probably has a back-up floppy diskette.

-- A few "Famous Last Words" about Computers --

Everything that can be invented has been invented.
  [Charles H. Duell, commissioner, U.S. Patent Office, 1899]

I think there is a worldwide market for maybe five computers.
  [Thomas J. Watson, chairman of IBM, 1943]

Computers in the future may weigh no more than 1.5 tons.
  [*Popular Mechanics*, forecasting new technology, 1949]

Data processing is a fad that won't last out the year.
  [Editor of business books for Prentice Hall, 1957]

But what is it good for?
  [an engineer at the Advanced Computing Systems Division, IBM; commenting on the development of the microchip, 1968]

There is no reason anyone would want a computer in their home.
  [Ken Olson, founder of Digital Equipment Corp., 1977]

Murphy's Military Definitions
for
Infantry

Warriors, pay attention! These combat definitions are crucial need-to-know material for the world's elite all-terrain combatants, the ***Infantry***. Basically, these definitions are "Grunt Stuff."

But, all you aviation types, this information also is important for you. Do you know the official military definition of *Cranial-Rectal Inversion Syndrome*? *Combat Experience*? *Bravery*? How about *Scrounge*? Do you remember the exact military meaning of the word, *Marriage*? How about *Mail Buoy Watch*?

All of those definitions are here, and they apply to all warriors. But they are absolutely essential for all of the supremely skilled population control specialists, the Grunts.

Following this list, Murphy has compiled an additional concise listing of military ***Aviation*** definitions. All Grunts should take a quick look at the aviation list, too. Yet, Murphy has a few stern words of caution! Grunts who read the aviation list more than twice will *never* agree to ride in a helicopter again.

Detailed below are Murphy's Military Definitions with which all warriors, especially the elite Grunt assassins, must be familiar:

Aircraft: (1) The precursor of the Frisbee. (2) The generic name for any noisy heavier-than-air flying contraption. (3) The most unreliable and most perilous means of travel on Earth.

Aircraft Carrier: The biggest, most expensive, slowest-moving, most explosive-filled, and most lucrative bull's-eye on Earth.

Airman: (1) A flaccid civilian detainee in the U.S. Air Force. (2) A pitiful chair-borne public assistance program reject. (3) A person whose lack of initiative, intellect, and physical stamina renders him incapable of finding employment in the private sector.

ALICE: (1) In *theory*, a possible good-time companion on leave or liberty. (2) In *reality*, not much fun in the deep end of the pool.

Ammo Dump: A place you should avoid during incoming mortar, rocket, or artillery fire -- even if it is a deep hole.

Armored Vehicle: The generic name for any heavy mobile steel conveyance that attracts armor-piercing incendiary rounds.

Artillery: A weapon designed to kill or maim as many of the enemy and his evil cohorts as possible and restore cave-dwelling as an acceptable way of life in the former enemy territory.

Ashore: The nebulous Department of the Navy term that means anywhere in the air, on land, or at sea -- except on base.

Ballistic: A characteristic of First Sergeants and Sergeants Major.

Bayonet: (1) A weapon of last resort. (2) A very poor choice of weapons to take to a firefight (the guy with the *bullets* will win).

Bayonet Fighting Expert: A warrior who knows that the Vertical Buttstroke is not a sexual technique.

Beachhead: The guaranteed bull's-eye for enemy mortars, artillery fire, and aerial bombardment.

BLT: (1) A lethal amphibious force. (2) Something that can not be ordered in any restaurant.

Board of Inquiry: A devious and spurious group of staff pogues who, given enough time and data, can prove anything.

Bravery: In common usage, a synonym for stupidity.

Brig (or Stockade): (1) An exceptionally poor choice for military lodging accommodations. (2) For all macho warriors, an *even worse* choice if the rest of their unit is in combat.

Brown-Bagger: (1) A well-intentioned warrior who has stumbled into the dark and evil snake-pit of marriage. (2) A term derived from the small *brown paper lunch bag* carried by married warriors, who can no longer afford to buy their own meals.

Carry On: A verbal order which means *resume doing nothing.*

Chinese Fire Drill: A time consuming group endeavor noteworthy for its absence of coordination and purpose.

Cinderella Liberty: A devious and despicable staff pogue ruse designed to encourage sobriety among warriors.

Close: A near-miss, a matter of *dire* concern in the related arts of (1) horseshoe throwing and (2) grenade tossing.

Close Air Support: A good thing to have if it is not *too* close.

College Campus: A place where the pitiful apostles of *political correctness* usually outnumber advocates of principle and honor.

Combat: What you are definitely in when you have run out of everything except the bad guys.

Combat Breakfast: Two aspirins, two cups of coffee (if available), a quick prayer, and a quick puke.

Combat Experience: The sum of your combat mistakes.

Combat Pay: (1) A flawed concept. (2) A premise which allows the government to *save money* by temporarily paying you *more money* in anticipation of your expedited demise.

Communism: (1) An ideology embraced by Marx, Engels, and other ignorami. (2) A form of socialism designed to impoverish any governmental entity. (3) A concept that would only work in Heaven, where it is not needed, and in Hell, where it is already established. (4) An easy way to raise suffering to a higher level.

Computer: (1) An electro-mechanical marvel, the operation of which is far beyond the intelligence level of the intended military user. (2) The primary cause of profanity among warriors.

Conclusion: Your best guess when you get tired of thinking.

Corpsman (or Medic):   In combat, a good man to buddy-up with.

Cranial-Rectal Inversion Syndrome: (1) A debilitating staff pogue illness. (2) A progressive and degenerative malaise. (3) A chronic mental paralysis believed by medical experts to result from a despicable staff practice too uncouth to describe.

Critical Terrain: Terrain which, if not grabbed or camped out on, will make you the *screwee* in offensive or defensive warfare.

D-Day: The day before which your insurance documents and your Last Will and Testament should be completed.

Death Before Dishonor: The most popular tattoo among warriors.

Defilade: When the shooting starts, the best position to be in.

Demilitarized Zone: A zone that should be, but usually is not.

Diplomacy: The art of explaining to the bad guys the manner and certainty of their impending demise if they fail to surrender.

Drill Instructor (or Drill Sergeant):   A maniacal, sadistic, extremist psychopath whose name you will never forget.

Field Day: A despised indoor non-athletic activity.

Fighting Hole: (1) Formerly called a *foxhole*. (2) Currently the technical name for a small military *hiding hole*.

Flex: A really cool-sounding and non-doctrinal term to explain how your unit will maneuver, under fire, from one battlefield location to another, when no one has a clue.

<u>Fool</u>: A warrior who still believes in fighting fair.

<u>Forward Air Controller</u>: (1) A "FAC," pronounced *fack*. (2) An unfortunate former pilot. (3) A devious person who must be closely watched (warriors interested in longevity should dive in a deep hole the instant their FAC begins chatting on his radio, for smoke and loud noise often follows).

<u>Four-Wheel-Drive</u>: A motor vehicle capability which enables one to get stuck in the mud at more remote and inaccessible locations.

<u>Geneva Convention</u>: A symposium of civilians who made up rules which warriors must follow in war -- unless no one is watching.

<u>Good Judgement</u>: Mental decision-making capacity derived from experience, which is derived from *bad* judgment.

<u>Grunt</u>: (1) A professional assassin. (2) An infantryman. (3) The sole reason for the existence of helicopters. (4) An indispensable element of the United States' Foreign Policy. (5) A warrior who will go anywhere at any time and destroy whatever he is ordered to destroy -- as long as he is allowed to sing obscene songs, kick cats, drink, brawl, embellish War Stories beyond recognition, and corrupt members of the opposite sex.

<u>Gulf War</u>: Four days of target practice in the land of sand, c 1991.

<u>Gungy</u>: An enlightened, euphoric, gung-ho state of mind.

<u>H-Hour</u>: The most introspective time of day.

<u>Head (or Latrine)</u>: In times of utter confusion, the small room in which you *still* should know what you are doing.

<u>Hero</u>: An illustrious term that all warriors apply to themselves (in the club after the fourth drink).

<u>Heroism</u>: A trait often displayed in combat after one has run out of all other viable options.

<u>Hey-diddle-diddle</u>: With reference to a proposed assault, (1) words which describe an absence of analytical thought, or (2) an offensive warfare tactic which guarantees an 80% or higher casualty rate.

<u>HMMWV, Humvee, Hummer, or whatever</u>: The western world's most expensive four-wheel-drive military or civilian play-toy.

<u>Latrine</u>: (see "Head")

<u>LAV</u>: (1) A small motorized conveyance with a big identity crisis. (2) A younger brother to a tank. (3) A thin-skinned steel box primarily useful as a crematorium for its occupants.

<u>LCAC</u>: (1) A huge 50 knot flying carpet. (2) A magical machine that defies gravity and all known laws of physics.

<u>LHA</u>: The official military acronym for Luxury Hotel Afloat.

<u>M-2 Bradley Fighting Vehicle</u>: (1) A comfortable conveyance for Grunts. (2) A dangerous steel box (think, *target*) which should be avoided like the bubonic plague during a tank battle.

<u>M-9 Service Pistol</u>: A firearm which -- if it is all you have in a firefight -- you *quickly* should exchange for a belt-fed weapon.

<u>M-16A2 Rifle</u>: A 5.56mm magazine fed, gas operated, air cooled, shoulder fired weapon -- manufactured by the *lowest bidder*.

<u>M-18A1 Claymore Mine</u>: A directional antipersonnel mine upon the side of which -- after deployment in combat -- you fervently hope you can not read the words, "Front, Toward Enemy."

<u>M-203, 40mm Grenade Launcher</u>: A single shot, breech loaded, pump action, shoulder fired mini-bomb launcher for which a tactical nuclear round would be an excellent idea.

<u>M-240G Machine Gun</u>: A heavy 7.6mm automatic weapon that you hope someone, *other than yourself*, has to carry.

<u>Maggie's Drawers</u>: (1) For all American Warriors, the only set of red drawers they *never* want to see. (2) An embarrassing insult.

<u>Mail Buoy Watch</u>: (1) A crucial nocturnal assignment for all new and useless U.S. Navy ensigns. (2) An aquatic snipe hunt.

<u>Map</u>: An archaic land navigation aid which is totally useless on the modern-day battlefield (unless all of your batteries have died).

<u>Marine</u>: (1) An unfortunate person who lacked the intelligence to get in the Air Force, the skills to get in the Navy, or the common sense to settle for the Army. (2) A member of a group of misfits collectively known as *Uncle Sam's Misguided Children*. (3) A person for whom all reading and writing test requirements have been permanently waived, and for whom "Ooo-rah!" is a sufficient verbal response to any question from a superior.

<u>Marriage</u>: (1) Not a military term. (2) A civil snake-pit into which well-intentioned warriors sometimes stumble. (3) The tragic result of trying to *think* with the wrong part of one's anatomy. (4) A progressive three-ring circus: engagement <u>ring</u>, wedding <u>ring</u>, and suff<u>ering</u>. (5) The number one cause of divorce.

<u>Medal</u>: (1) The generic name for any one of a multitude of eye-catching uniform trinkets. (2) The shiny doo-dads that aggressive warriors always want more of -- *exclusive* of the Purple Heart.

<u>Medic</u>: (see "Corpsman")

<u>MEU</u>: Next to a Class 5 hurricane or a 700 foot high tsunami, the most lethal force on planet Earth.

<u>MEU (SOC)</u>: A lethal force *more* destructive than a Class 5 hurricane or a 700 foot high tsunami.

<u>Mines</u>: The generic name for all Equal Opportunity Weapons.

<u>Mortar</u>: In combat, the weapon you would least like to carry.

MOUT: (1) Exclusive of the north pole and south pole, the last environment on Earth where wise warriors want to fight. (2) An environment where discretion *really* is the better part of valor.

MPC: (1) Funny-money. (2) As worthless as "Monopoly" money.

Napalm: (1) Incindi-gel. (2) An excellent area support weapon.

Nomex: A synthetic fiber designed to burst into flame at moderate temperatures and be impossible to extinguish.

Ode to Naivety (posthumous): "Often wrong, but never in doubt."

Old Corps, The: (1) The era of the M-1 Garand. (2) The era when John Wayne was still on active duty. (3) The era when the Chinese Army did not have enough rowboats to invade Taiwan. (4) Or, any era before *any* of the above.

Payback: An inspirational experience *if* you survive it.

Peace Is Our Profession: The pacifist motto (*really*, believe it or not) for the Strategic Air Command of the U.S. Air Force.

Perimeter Defense: What Gen. George A. Custer, USA, and his Seventh Cavalry should have established at the Little Big Horn on 25 June 1876, shortly before their untimely demise.

PFM: The military acronym for the comprehensive, easy-to-understand, non-technical explanation for why a complex system functioned as it did -- when you do not have a clue.

Pogey Bait: (1) The most nutritious of the four major food groups. (2) The instant energy source of choice, especially when one's cholesterol level is too low.

Political Correctness Counsellor: (1) A civilian advisor who is depriving a village, somewhere, of its idiot. (2) A person who would be out of his depth in a parking lot puddle. (3) An utter ignoramus, a wimp, a hand-wringing sniveling weakling.

<u>Preparation Fire</u>: (1) Commonly called *prep-fire*. (2) Smoke and loud noise designed to promote unwarranted confidence among members of the waiting assault force.

<u>Professional Reading List</u>: A list of inspirational books that **does not** include (1) *Fighter Aces of the Iraqi Air Force* and (2) *Under Fire as a Combat Photographer*, by Albert Gore Jr.

<u>Purple Heart</u>: The *least desirable* medal awarded to warriors by the United States of America.

<u>R & R</u>: (1) In *theory*, the standard military acronym for "Rest and Recuperation." (2) In *reality*, usually "I & I."

<u>Radio</u>: When in a firefight, a useless electronic suggestion box.

<u>Rate of Fire</u>: (1) The *theoretical* number of rounds an automatic weapon can fire in one minute. (2) A *meaningless* term because the weapon would melt if any idiot ever tried it.

<u>Recon (or Special Forces, or SEAL)</u>: (1) The *stealth* version of the basic U.S. Marine, U.S. Army soldier, or U.S. Navy sailor. (2) A warpainted assassin who prefers to fight with his knife, his bayonet, his E-tool, his teeth, and his fists, just to conserve ammunition.

<u>Reconnaissance by Fire</u>: A noisy technique used on patrol when you can not see through the thick bushes.

<u>REMF (spoken, *ree-miff*)</u>: The official military acronym for Rear-Echelon-Mother-[expletive].   The term used by all combat infantrymen and aircrews to describe military personnel in safe administrative and support roles, far from the fighting -- even though such persons secretly may be envied.

<u>Roach Coach</u>: A mobile civilian-owned mercenary distributor of diarrhea, heartburn, and other symptoms of gastrointestinal distress.

<u>Rug Dance</u>: (1) A rhythmic shuffling endeavor that requires no partner. (2) A spirited form of dancing during an extraordinarily

one-sided chat with one's irate superior.

Rules of Engagement: The childish rules that you and your fellow warriors can *claim* you followed to the letter -- if you make sure to kill all of the bad guys who might have claimed otherwise.

Sailor: (1) A primitive pre-Neanderthal life form. (2) A deck ape. (3) A nautical paint-picker. (4) A member of the under-class of dark, slimy, pitiful, squid-like creatures, most of whom have been banished to their natural habitat in the murky depths of the ocean where normal human beings do not have to associate with them.

Scrounge: (1) A *verb*; meaning to obtain by a devious method. (2) A *noun*; meaning a highly skilled warrior who is adept at obtaining, by devious methods, virtually anything from crates of frozen steaks to tactical atomic weapons. (3) A comshaw artist.

Secure: A term with differing implications. For example, if asked to *secure a building*, the following actions will be taken:

  U.S. Navy: Turn out the lights and shut the door.

  U.S. Air Force: Set up a three year lease with an option to buy.

  U.S. Army: Occupy the structure, post a guard, and permit only persons with proper identification to enter.

  U.S. Marine Corps: Conduct a "hey-diddle-diddle" assault to kill all innocent women and children occupants.

Short-arm Inspection: A despised practice rendered obsolete by the miracles of modern medicine.

Slopchute: (1) A geedunk that serves libations. (2) A facility not noted for stocking nutrients of the four major food groups.

Smoking Lamp: A nonexistent lamp that can nonetheless be *lit*.

SNAFU / FUBAR / SAPFU: Acronyms, not words, which are

listed in ascending order of implied ineptitude and/or stupidity.

<u>Snake and Nape</u>: In a protracted battle, a wonderful thing to find that your aviation brothers-in-arms have plenty of.

<u>Sniper's Motto</u>: "Reach out and touch someone."

<u>Soldier</u>: (1) The common name for a member of the world's largest bureaucracy, the U.S. Army. (2) A person easily recognized by (a) his trousers, which are too short; (b) his hat, which is too large; (c) the huge pockets on his clothing, in which he can warm his dainty little hands; and (d) the vast assortment of emblems, crests, badges, and shiny dangling doo-dads that adorn his clothing, which is similar to that of a Greyhound bus driver.

<u>Special Forces</u>: (see "Recon")

<u>Stockade</u>: (see "Brig")

<u>Straight Scoop</u>: *Factual* information, as opposed to a new PFC or Airman or Seaman who reports, "I just got the word . . . ."

<u>Stuff</u>: A nebulous term that can refer to (1) a tangible thing or to (2) a situation, condition, or process, as exemplified below:

A: *This is rough **stuff***. Typical statement of an Air Force NCO while driving his air-conditioned sedan, from his air-conditioned office to his air-conditioned quarters, **in the rain**.

B: *This is really rough **stuff***. Typical statement of an Army Ranger, weapon at sling arms and carrying a 30 pound pack, after jumping from an aircraft and marching eight miles to the ***wrong*** map coordinates or rally point, **in the rain**.

C: *This is horrible **stuff***. Typical statement of a Navy SEAL, lying in the mud with his 40 pound pack, weapon in hand, after jumping from an aircraft, swimming a mile to shore, and crawling to the ***wrong*** objective, **in the rain**.

D: *I love this **stuff**.* Typical statement of a Marine Recon, up to his eyeballs in a vermin-infested swamp with his 60 pound pack, a weapon in each hand; after jumping from an aircraft, swimming two miles to shore, killing several alligators while negotiating the swamp, and attacking the ***wrong*** village and killing all the unarmed women and children, **in the rain**.

Sucking Chest Wound: Nature's way of telling you to slow down.

Supporting Fire: An excellent thing to witness *if* it is yours.

Surrender: Despicable conduct that wimps often attempt to engage in, *especially* if they are into (1) masochism or (2) cold rice balls.

Tank: (1) A heavy steel box crammed full of explosives. (2) An efficient crematorium for its talented crew. (3) Otherwise, a monument to the inaccuracy of direct fire.

Target of Opportunity: A bad thing to become, or be mistaken for.

Terrorist: A freedom fighter with a different perspective.

TRICARE: A sick joke -- on you and your family.

U.S. Air Force: (1) A government-funded amateur *flying club*. (2) An organization composed of prima donna aeronautical wannabes who were unable to find employment in the private sector.

U.S. Army: (1) A government ***gun club***. (2) A large bureaucracy which provides free housing and remedial training for prison parolees and Rambo wannabes who have been unable to cope with the day-to-day pressures of society.

U.S. Marine Corps: (1) A government-mandated ***penal institution*** for societal misfits. (2) A federal rehabilitation program devoted to the welfare of a motley collection of incorrigible psychopaths commonly known as "Jarheads" (whatever *Jarheads* may be).

U.S. Navy: (1) A government-sponsored aquatic ***cruise service***.

(2) An effective way to quarantine the slovenly under-class of mentally degenerate persons far out at sea, where they are unable to mate and cause damage to the world's gene pool.

<u>Vampire</u>: The common name for either (1) a this-is-no-drill *enemy weapon* or a (2) nocturnal Transylvanian blood-sucker.

<u>Vietnam</u>: A place where it *did too* get cold at night.

<u>Vietnam War</u>: A conflict in which hundreds of American Warriors earned medals for extraordinary valor in combat every day, and in which -- from time to time -- a few were actually awarded.

<u>War</u>: In general, the unfolding of miscalculations.

<u>Warrior</u>: (1) A street-legal assassin. (2) A romping, stomping, devil-may-care purveyor of death and destruction. (3) A rough, overbearing, self-centered psychopathic killer by day, lover by night, and drunkard by choice. (4) One who can curse for ten minutes without repeating a word. (5) One who knows that "Kill, sir!" is the proper response to any and all questions from superiors. (6) One who thinks that "sodomy" and "politically correct" should fall into the same sub-chapter in the UCMJ.

Murphy's Military Definitions
for
Aviation

Heads up, you aviation types! If ***staying alive*** in aerial combat is of interest to you, this is crucial scientific stuff.

Be forewarned! Even in peacetime, military aircraft have a penchant for perverse and evil habits. They come unglued in flight. They run out of gas. They butt heads with mountains in the dark. All of these idiosyncrasies adversely affect the longevity of those who ride or fly in these flimsy contraptions. And do not even *mention* helicopters! If the Grunts knew all that Murphy knows about helicopters, they would never ride in one again.

In this chapter, Murphy will define the things that keep us alive, or kill us, such as *Gravity, Hydroplane,* and *Dead Reckoning.* Also, *Pucker Factor* is scientifically explained. Are you confused about the *Bang-Stare-Red Theory? Chicken Plate? Retreating Blade Stall?* If so, this chapter is for you.

Are there any Grunt assassins who desire insight into modern military aviation, the most perilous mode of transportation on Earth? If so, they should read on. They may conclude that early retirement is not such a bad idea:

A-Model: (1) An underpowered experimental aircraft prototype. (2) A primitive contraption you should *never* ride or fly in.

Accident Investigation Board: *Six men* who take *six months* reviewing what the deceased crew did during the last *six seconds* of their lives (in the rain, at night, in the mountains, under fire).

Acey-Deucey: A competitive exercise designed to weed out any pilots who lack the killer instinct necessary for combat.

ADF: An aircraft navigation instrument of last resort.

<u>Aeronautics</u>: (1) Neither an industry nor a science. (2) A miracle.

<u>Aircraft Nomenclature and Descriptions</u>:

-- Most Common Military Helicopters --

<u>AH-1W/Z Super Cobra</u>: (1) A primitive flying machine unable to adapt to *wheel* technology. (2) A mini-attack helicopter that added more rotor blades to *try* to look like an Apache.

<u>AH-64D Apache Longbow</u>: The least favorite weapon of all bad guys who are tank crewmen.

<u>CH-46E Sea Knight</u>: A totally unreliable and antiquated flying machine known by its survivors as the "shuddering [expletive]." Just say a *Hail Mary* and climb aboard.

<u>CH-47D Chinook</u>: The big, bold, and bad combat helicopter that its baby brother, the CH-46E, should have been.

<u>CH-53E Sea Stallion</u>: Proof of the concept that, if you keep on adding rotor blades and engines, *anything* will eventually fly.

<u>UH-1N Huey</u>: An old primeval *skid-mounted* flying machine which was built before man's invention of *wheels*.

<u>UH-60L Blackhawk</u>: The same thing as a Huey on steroids.

-- Most Common Military Fixed-Wing Aircraft --

<u>A-10 Thunderbolt</u>: A flying warthog with a titanium bathtub.

<u>AV-8B Harrier</u>: A really cool-looking jet VTOL/STOL attack aircraft with *illusions* of also being a fighter.

<u>B-52H Stratofortress</u>: (1) A big fifty-plus year old strategic bomber in which, after four engines have failed, you still have four more that have not. (2) Proof of the hypothesis that, if you glued enough jet engines onto it, even a brick could fly.

C-130A/J Hercules: (1) An aircraft designed in the 1940s, in service in the 1950s, and still being *built* 50 years later. (2) A *normally* sedate aircraft, the AC-130H/U Spectre/Spooky version of which is nothing for the enemy to trifle with.

F-15A/E Eagle: A sleek and speedy aircraft whose most useful capability is to astound civilian air-show attendees with a nifty vertical vanishing act.

F-16C Fighting Falcon: A concession to economics; the only modern-day U.S. combat aircraft with less than two engines.

F-117A Nighthawk: The aircraft with the smallest and lightest bomb load capability in the entire U.S. Armed Forces.

F/A-18E/F Super Hornet: A sleek supersonic machine primarily useful for enemy surface-to-air-missile (SAM) target practice.

MV-22 Osprey: A high-tech bird of *prey*, in which you *pray*.

Air Medal: A military award bestowed upon pilots and aircrewmen who blunder into a perilous situation in combat and, through *dumb luck* alone, manage to survive.

Airspeed: Expressed in knots, the speed of a military aircraft relative to the air mass through which it travels (deduct 40% when listening to civilian pilots or REMFs).

All-Weather Close Air Support: Superior and overwhelming aerial fire support for infantrymen, available 24 hours a day *except* (1) during inclement weather and (2) at night.

"Alpha-Mike-Foxtrot": The common verbal farewell (1) to any despicable person, or (2) to an enemy you have just shot down.

Alternate Airport: Any airport 50 or more miles beyond the maximum range of an IFR aircraft.

Altimeter: A barometric pressure sensing device that indicates height above *sea level* (consequently, it is *useless over land*).

Radar Altimeter: (1) Better than the plain altimeter. (2) An electronic sensing device that indicates height above either the land or the sea (usually works OK, unless you are flying IFR toward the side of a steep mountain).

Attitude Indicator: A cockpit instrument that had *better be working* while flying IFR or flying at night.

Autorotation: An inexplicable and terrifying helicopter maneuver that you only get *one chance* to try. Ironically, the higher you are when the terror begins, the better. (also, see "Pucker Factor")

Back Side of the Power Curve: (1) A dreaded world of *slow flight* defined by obscure laws of aerodynamics and physics that no one understands. (2) The side of the curve you do not want to be on.

Bang-Stare-Red Theory: A time-tested aeronautical truth which substantiates that (1) the louder a sudden *bang* in an aircraft, the quicker the pilot's eyes will be drawn to the gauges, and (2) the longer the pilot stares at the gauges, the quicker the needles will move from the green arcs into the red arcs.

Bank: The generic name for the civilian institution that holds the lien on cars driven by military pilots and aircrewmen.

Barrel Roll: The preferred method of moving beer containers.

Carburetor Icing: In piston-powered manned aircraft or UAVs, a phenomenon which occurs when the fuel tanks mysteriously become full of air. (also, see "Engine Failure")

CAVU: (1) The stuff aeronautical dreams are made of. (2) What Heaven surely must be like.

Chicken Plate: (1) Standard combat attire for helicopter crews. (2) Something that can not be ordered in a restaurant.

Chip Detector Light: A *really* evil thing when you are flying IFR.

Cloud: A beautiful fluffy opaque meteorological phenomenon in which mountains frequently lurk.

Cluster Bombing: An aerial bombardment technique that is 100% accurate, because the bombs *always* hit the ground in clusters.

Combat, Aerial: What you are in when those pretty little *orange baseballs* are zipping past, and sometimes through, your aircraft.

Copilot: A useless person *until* he spots closing traffic at 12 o'clock (after which he is an ignoramus for not seeing it sooner).

Crab: The squadron Operations Officer.

Crash: Nature's way of warning military pilots and aircrewmen to watch their airspeed.

Cruise Box: (1) A large footlocker that is loaded aboard an aircraft by its crew chief/loadmaster. (2) A useless heavy box, the weight of which reduces the passenger load by two Grunts.

Dead Reckoning: (1) You reckon correctly, or you are. (2) The least preferred method of aerial navigation.

Drag: A highly intoxicated male aviator who has left the bar in a drunken stupor while wearing a woman's coat by mistake.

Emergency Extraction: (1) What helicopter crews have to do in combat -- usually at night, for some obscure and dreaded reason. (2) A sure remedy for "tired blood."

Emergency Night Medevac (by helicopter): Either (1) a nocturnal emergency flight to save the life of a wounded brother-in-arms, or (2) a guaranteed cure for constipation, or (3) both.

Engine Failure: A phenomenon which occurs when the fuel tanks of an aircraft become full of air. (also, see "Carburetor Icing")

Experienced Crew: An aircraft crew that has survived long enough to recognize a mistake when they make it again.

FAA Motto: "We are not happy until you are not happy."

Famous Last Words (above and beyond all others): "Don't worry about the weight, it'll fly."

Firewall: The metallic structure in an aircraft which is designed to direct flame and smoke into the cockpit.

Flying: (1) Something difficult to do without feathers. (2) The common term for the illusion of immortality. (3) The ability to throw yourself through the sky and avoid hitting the ground.

   Night Flying: The same thing as *day* flying, except that you can not see where you are going.

FOD-Burger: An inedible substance, the ingestion of which will hopefully be discovered *prior* to attempted flight.

Fuel: A limited resource without which the crew and passengers in an aircraft (1) become pedestrians, or (2) become deceased.

G-Suit: Clothing designed to prevent inappropriate aerial napping.

Glide Distance: Half the distance from an aircraft in distress to the nearest suitable emergency landing area.

Glider: A complex and sophisticated aircraft, the fuel tanks of which have unexpectedly become full of air.

GPS: (1) The aviation acronym for "Going Perfectly Straight." (2) Also, the common name for the electronic black-box gizmo that lets you go perfectly straight.

Gravity: The primary cause of most military aircraft crashes. It may not be fair, but (1) it is the law, (2) it is not subject to repeal, and (3) it is forever.

Headwind: (1) The result of any attempt to stretch fuel. (2) A meteorological occurrence on all lengthy over-water flights.

Helicopter: The generic name for a heavier-than-air, vertical take-off, flying machine comprised of thousands of parts, all of which rapidly spin in opposite directions, constantly striving to tear themselves apart, and often succeeding.

HIGE: The best place for a helicopter crew to hover.

HOGE: (1) A stupid *thing* for a helicopter crew to do. (2) An invisible and mysterious aerodynamic *capability* that helicopter crews want to *have*, but never want to *use*.

Hovering: A type of flying practiced by helicopter crews that have no specific place to go.

Hydroplane: A flying machine designed to land on wet runways.

IFR: (1) Not nearly as good as VFR. (2) In common day-to-day usage, the acronym for "I follow railroads." (3) A tricky method of flying by needle and horoscope.

Instrument Flying: (1) An unnatural act. (2) Not a good idea. (3) How you fly when you can not fly like you want to fly.

Jet Aircraft: The most expensive way to convert JP-8 into noise.

Landing: A technique for falling out of the sky with style.

> *Good* Landing: A landing after which all of the aircraft crewmembers can walk away without assistance.

> *Great* Landing: A landing after which (1) the aircraft doors will still open and (2) the aircraft can be salvaged.

Landing Gear Handle: The cockpit handle that a smart pilot will place in the *down* position immediately after a gear-up landing.

<u>Lean Mixture</u>: Non-alcoholic beer.

<u>*Rich* Mixture</u>: The type of beverage you order at the *other guy's* promotion party.

<u>MARCAD/NAVCAD</u>: A wartime USN/USMC flight training program which produces (1) *twice* the pilot at (2) *half* the price.

<u>"Mayday! Mayday! Mayday!"</u>: A verbal notice that prayer, while it may not help, is still an excellent idea.

<u>Meatball</u>: For military pilots, a longevity-related phenomenon to be closely watched, not eaten.

<u>Mile High Club</u>: (1) If you do not know, you are not in it. (2) A club that requires co-conspirators of the opposite sex.

<u>Minimums</u>: After crashing and surviving, the altitude below which you must swear you did not descend while flying IFR.

<u>Nanosecond</u>: The time delay built into stall warning systems.

<u>Navigation, Aerial</u>: The scientific process used by an aircrew to get from Point A to Point B, while *trying* to get to Point C.

<u>OBE</u>: The untenable condition that occurs when an aircraft travels faster than the brain of its pilot.

<u>Pilot</u>: A confused person who (1) talks about women when he is flying, and who (2) talks about flying when he is with a woman.

<u>Precision Bombing</u>: Hi-tech and smart-weapon aerial bombardment accurate to within plus/minus seven miles (more or less).

<u>Preflight Planning</u>: A time consuming exercise in futility.

<u>Pucker Factor</u>: (1) The scientific formula (T x I x R over H) which determines the contraction force of the *Gluteus Maximus* muscles. (2) The common term for the *degree of contraction* of

these muscles in times of dire peril.   (3) In *real world* aviation language, the mathematical calculation which determines the amount of seat cushion that will be sucked into the rectum of pilots and aircrewmen who are under enemy fire.   On a 1-to-500 ascending scale, it may be determined as follows: **T** (number of *tracers* headed your way) x **I** (your *interest* in staying alive) x **R** (your *rate* of descent) divided by **H** (your *height* above ground).   Murphy's Technical Note: for mathematical computation purposes, each incoming *missile* equates to *five tracers.*

Range: Approximately 30 miles beyond the point where all fuel tanks will become full of air.

Retreating Blade Stall: (1) The aerodynamic nemesis of helicopters that fly too fast before crashing. (2) Something *really* repulsive. (3) The primary cause of insomnia among helicopter crewmen.

"Roger": A radio transmission used by pilots who are unsure of the proper radio response.

Roll: A design priority for all transport helicopters.

Running Take-off: A nifty practice maneuver. But if a helicopter *has* to do it, you do not want to be riding in it.

SAR: A type of mission you hope you are not the objective of.

Separation: The condition achieved when two or more aircraft fail to collide in flight.

"Sierra-Hotel": (1) What you say in correspondence, or in mixed company, when you can not say what you *really* want to say. (2) The socially appropriate but "politically incorrect" synonym for: Outstanding! Aggressive! Exemplary! Supremely skilled!

Single Engine Capability: A "level flight" capability which most multi-engine aircraft have, *until* they try to land.

Slip: Flimsy civilian-style undergarments worn by some women.

Spoilers: Members of the Accident Investigation Board.

Stall: A technique for thwarting proposals of matrimony.

Tail Rotor: (1) The helicopter rotor which is magnetically drawn toward trees, stumps, poles, wires, and other obstructions to flight. (2) The fragile little rear rotor that -- unlike the main rotor, which can chop down hickory trees -- will self-destruct if it hits anything bigger than a honey-bee.

Tail Wind: The result of eating beans and other leguminous foods.

Terminal Forecast: A complex horoscope with lots of numbers.

Thunderstorm: (1) Mother Nature's way of saying, "Up yours!" (2) The common term for *cumulo-securus* clouds.

Translational Lift: (1) For helicopter crews, a *very* good thing. (2) A phenomenon attributed to black magic. (3) An aerodynamic wonderland that vanishes, unfortunately, when you try to land.

Turn and Slip Indicator: A cockpit instrument of no use to pilots.

Useful Load: The total volumetric capacity of a military aircraft, regardless of the gross weight of the aircraft.

VFR: (1) The meteorological conditions under which members of an aircrew can see what they collided with. (2) The rules a pilot can "declare" if the proposed *IFR* procedure is too complex.

   Special VFR: The rules a pilot can "declare" when *regular* VFR simply will not work.

Weather: Next to *gravity*, the biggest cause of aircraft crashes.

"Whiskey-Tango-Foxtrot?": (1) A *polite* radio or ICS query. (2) An in-flight question most often voiced when the crew of another aircraft is engaged in exceptionally stupid conduct.

--Now --

Get ready for
a ***serious*** look
at the
Warrior Heritage
and
Combat Culture
of the
U.S. Armed Forces

PART THREE

Heritage
of the
American Warrior

A *<u>Serious</u>* Look
at the
Warrior Heritage
of the
U.S. Armed Forces

Anthems of the Armed Forces and the National Anthem

-- United States Army --

No military anthem of the United States has undergone more change than the Army anthem. First came *The Caisson Song*, later followed by *The Army Goes Rolling Along*.

In 1908 the U.S. Army stationed 1stLt. Edmund L. Gruber with the 5th Field Artillery in the Philippines. In that bygone era the field artillery "caissons" were pulled by teams of mules. While accompanying an artillery detachment on primitive roads through the rugged mountains, Gruber heard the section chief repeatedly yell, "**Keep 'em rolling!**"

Later, Gruber and his friends composed an inspirational song. On a guitar, Gruber strummed a peppy up-beat melody. William Bryden and Robert Danford kicked in and helped Gruber write the lyrics to *The Caisson Song*. The words relate to the mule-drawn artillery caissons "rolling along." The new song became immensely popular with the artillerymen in the Philippines, especially at Happy Hour time. Soldiers returning to the United States carried the song with them, and soon each of the six regiments of the U.S. Army Field Artillery unofficially adopted it:

The Caisson Song

Over hill, over dale,
As we hit the dusty trail,
And those caissons go rolling along.
In and out, hear them shout,
Counter march and right about,
And those caissons go rolling along. [Refrain]

[Refrain]

> Then it's hi! hi! hee!
> In the field artillery,
> Shout out your numbers loud and strong,
> For where e'er you go,
> You will always know,
> That those caissons go rolling along.

In the storm, in the night,
Action left or action right,
See those caissons go rolling along;
Limber front, limber rear,
Prepare to mount your cannoneer,
And those caissons go rolling along. [Refrain]

Was it high, was it low,
Where the hell did that one go?
As those caissons go rolling along;
Was it left, was it right?
Now we won't get home tonight,
And those caissons go rolling along. [Refrain]

During World War I the Army hierarchy wanted a marching song. Noted bandmaster John Philip Sousa, erroneously thinking that *The Caisson Song* dated back to the Civil War era, made some minor changes to the words and tune and retitled it, *The U.S. Field Artillery March*. The song became popular with the Army and with the American public and sold almost a million copies. Shortly thereafter, Sousa learned that Gruber had written the song only a few years before. Sousa did the proper thing; he arranged for Gruber to get all of the credit and all monetary royalties.

In 1948 the Army conducted a contest to create an *official* Army song. The results were dismal, and no selection was made. Four years later the Army asked the music industry for help. Over 700 compositions poured in, but none had the kind of *magic* the Army sought. Finally a soldier, H.W. Arberg, hit paydirt. He kept the tune of *The Caisson Song*, but he wrote all-new lyrics to bring the ditty up to date. The Army knew a musical winner when it saw one and immediately adopted *The Army Goes Rolling Along*.

Yet, many die-hard Army veterans still revere the original classic, *The Caisson Song.* In countless bars and in military clubs on bases around the world, Happy Hour is often synonymous with spirited top-of-the-lungs renditions of "the caissons go rolling along!" Nonetheless, *The Army Goes Rolling Along* is now the official song of the United States Army:

The Army Goes Rolling Along

[Introduction]

> March along, sing our song, with the Army of the free,
> Count the brave, count the true, who have fought to victory,
> We're the Army and proud of our name!
> We're the Army and proudly proclaim:

First to fight for the right,
And to build the Nation's might,
And the Army goes rolling along.
Proud of all we have done,
Fighting 'till the battle's won,
And the Army goes rolling along. [Refrain]

[Refrain]

> Then it's Hi! Hi! Hey! The Army's on its way!
> Count off the cadence loud and strong,
> For where e'er we go, you will always know,
> That the Army goes rolling along.

Valley Forge, Custer's ranks,
San Juan Hill and Patton's tanks,
And the Army went rolling along,
Minute-men, from the start,
Always fighting from the heart,
And the Army goes rolling along. [Refrain]

Men in rags, men who froze,
Still that Army met its foes,
And the Army went rolling along,
Faith in God, then we're right,

And we'll fight with all our might,
As the Army goes rolling along. [Refrain]

-- United States Navy --

The Navy anthem has changed, too. The original anthem was written about the game of football, not about the Navy fleet.

Lt. Charles A. Zimmermann became the bandmaster of the Naval Academy Band in 1887. He began composing a musical march each year in honor of the Naval Academy graduating class.

In 1906, Alfred H. Miles suggested that the Academy needed a special "football" song for the upcoming Army-Navy football game. Miles, a Naval Academy midshipman, thought that their under-dog team needed music that would inspire them, a song that would "live forever." It seemed like a good idea to Zimmermann, so he composed a jaunty tune. Collaborating with Zimmermann, Miles wrote original lyrics for the two stanzas of *Anchors Aweigh*, a new Naval Academy football game "fight song":

Anchors Aweigh (original "football" lyrics)

Stand, Navy, down the field, sails set to the sky,
We'll never change our course, so, Army, you steer shy-y-y-y,
Roll up the score, Navy, Anchors Aweigh,
Sail, Navy, down the field, and sink the Army, sink the Army Grey.

Get underway, Navy, decks cleared for the fray,
We'll hoist true Navy Blue, so, Army, down your Grey-y-y-y,
Full speed ahead, Navy; Army, heave to,
Furl Black and Grey and Gold, and hoist the Navy, hoist the Navy Blue.

While the midshipmen sang, the Naval Academy Band played *Anchors Aweigh* at the annual Army-Navy football game in November 1906. For the first time in several years, Navy won the game. To celebrate their gridiron victory, the Naval Academy dedicated the new song to the entire Class of 1907. Later the U.S. Navy adopted it as the official Navy song.

The original song, written for the football game, contained lyrics intended to motivate the team. The words did not have much to do with the military responsibilities and wartime duties of the Navy. To correct this situation, George Lottman later penned replacement lyrics for the two original stanzas. The new lyrics made *Anchors Aweigh* an ideal nautical anthem for the Navy. Royal Lovell, a midshipman, wrote the final stanza in 1926.

The second stanza of these revised lyrics has evolved into the universally recognized and beloved musical icon of the United States Navy. And because the tune is unchanged, it remains the popular "fight song" of the Naval Academy football team:

Anchors Aweigh (revised lyrics)

Stand, Navy, out to sea; fight, our battle cry,
We'll never change our course, so vicious foe, steer shy-y-y-y,
Roll out the TNT, Anchors Aweigh,
Sail on to victory, and sink their bones to Davy Jones, hooray!

Anchors Aweigh, my boys, Anchors Aweigh,
Farewell to college joys, we sail at break of day-y-y-y,
Through our last night on shore, drink to the foam,
Until we meet once more, here's wishing you a happy voyage
    home.

Blue of the Seven Seas; Gold of God's great sun,
Let these our colors be, 'till all of time be done-n-n-n,
By Severn shore we learn, Navy's stern call:
Faith, courage, service true, with honor over, honor over all.

-- United States Marine Corps --

The oldest United States military anthem belongs to the United States Marine Corps. But the Marines are different. They do not have a song. Instead, they have a *hymn*.

The Marines' Hymn chronicles the military prowess of the Marine Corps. During the war with the Barbary Pirates in 1805, Lt. Presley O'Bannon led the Marine attack that captured the fortress at Derna on **"the shores of Tripoli."** During the Mexican

War, Marines led the bloody charge to seize Chapultepec Castle, the ancient "**halls of Montezuma**." Reversing these two phrases in the interest of euphony, an unknown author penned the first line of the world's most famous military anthem.

The hymn was in widespread use by the Marines and the American public by the mid-1800s. Yet, despite many attempts, no one was able to identify the author of the lyrics.

Various people made attempts to trace the origin of the *tune*. Col. A.S. McLemore, USMC, spent several years trying to track down the source. He wrote to the leader of the Marine Band, telling him that the tune originated from the comic opera *Genevieve de Barbant*, by Jaques Offenback. This opera was first presented at the Theatre de Bouffes Parisiens, in Paris, on 19 November 1859. But many others maintain that the tune has earlier roots in a Spanish folk song.

In 1929, *The Marines' Hymn* became the official anthem of the Marine Corps. Thirteen years later on 21 November 1942 the Marine Commandant approved a change in the words of the first stanza, fourth line. Because of the increasing use of aircraft in the Corps, the words were changed to "In the air, on land, and sea."

The "combat-and-victory" oriented theme and the peppy tune of the hymn made it famous worldwide. Sir Winston Churchill, British Prime Minister, became fascinated with the hymn. At official functions of state he often entertained guests by reciting, from memory, all three stanzas of *The Marines' Hymn*:

The Marines' Hymn

From the Halls of Montezuma,
To the Shores of Tripoli;
We fight our country's battles,
In the air, on land, and sea;
First to fight for right and freedom,
And to keep our honor clean;
We are proud to claim the title,
    Of United States Marines.

Our flag's unfurled to every breeze,
From dawn to setting sun;

We have fought in every clime and place,
Where we could take a gun;
In the snow of far-off northern lands,
And in sunny tropic scenes,
You will find us always on the job --
  The United States Marines.

Here's health to you and to our Corps,
Which we are proud to serve;
In many a strife we've fought for life,
And never lost our nerve;
If the Army and the Navy,
Ever look on Heaven's scenes,
They will find the streets are guarded,
  By United States Marines.

-- United States Air Force --

In the early 1900s the United States did not have an "Air Force." Instead, it had the new U.S. Army Air Corps, which had no unique anthem. The mainline Army's unofficial anthem at the time, *The Caisson Song*, was oriented toward mule-drawn ground artillery.

In 1938, *Liberty Magazine* sponsored a contest for an official song for the Army Air Corps. The magazine received 757 entries. A group of Army Air Corps wives was given the task of selecting the winning entry. They picked the submission of Robert M. Crawford, *Off We Go into the Wild Blue Yonder*. Crawford, an accomplished vocalist, introduced and sang the new song at the Cleveland Air Races on 2 September 1939.

Crawford had studied voice in France. He graduated from the prestigious Julliard School of Music, and he routinely gave concerts at Carnegie Hall and New York's illustrious St. Thomas Church. He flew a private airplane to concerts across the United States, and *Time Magazine* once called him the "Flying Baritone."

The U.S. Army Air Corps faded into history on 18 September 1947. The new U.S. Air Force absorbed the men and machines of their nation's air arm. The Air Force also adopted *Off We Go into the Wild Blue Yonder*. The last words of each stanza, "the Army Air Corps," were soon replaced with "the U.S. Air Force."

As a matter of interest, the musical score of *Off We Go'* was carried to the moon on 30 July 1971 aboard the Apollo 15 lunar module. With the aid of a tape recorder, the American astronauts broadcast *Off We Go'* to the world as the lunar module blasted off from the moon to dock with the orbiting command module.

"A Toast to the Host" is part of the Air Force song. This musical bridge, with a different melody and mood, serves as a solemn tribute to the members of the U.S. Air Force who have made the Supreme Sacrifice for their country:

Off We Go into the Wild Blue Yonder

Off we go into the wild blue yonder,
Climbing high into the sun;
Here they come zooming to meet our thunder,
At'em, boys, give'er the gun!
Down we dive spouting our flames from under,
Off with one hell-uv-a roar!
We live in fame or go down in flame,
Nothing can stop the U.S. Air Force!

Minds of men fashioned a crate of thunder,
Sent it high into the blue,
Hands of men blasted the world asunder,
How they live, God only knew,
Souls of men dreaming of skies to conquer,
Gave us wings ever to soar!
With scouts before and bombers galore,
Nothing can stop the U.S. Air Force!

[**Musical bridge**: "A Toast to the Host"]
Here's a toast to the host of those,
Who love the vastness of the sky;
To a friend we send the message,
Of his brother-men who fly.
We drink to those who gave their all of old,
Then down we roar to score the rainbow's pot of gold.
A toast to the host of men we boast, the U.S. Air Force!

Off we go into the wild blue yonder,
Keep the wings level and true;
If you'd live to be a gray haired wonder,
Keep your nose out of the blue!
Flying men guarding our nation's borders,
We'll be there followed by more,
In echelon we carry on,
Nothing can stop the U.S. Air Force!

-- United States of America --

Bitter territorial squabbles and trade disputes boiled over into war between the United States and Great Britain in 1812. Fighting on home ground, the United States won early victories. But by 1814, with Napoleon's Army defeated in Europe, Britain was able to turn its entire military juggernaut against the United States.

That summer the British invaded Washington, DC. They burned and ransacked the American capital. Then the invaders turned their war machine toward nearby Baltimore, a coastal city guarded by Fort McHenry on the Patapsco River inlet.

Adm. Alexander Cochrane, RN, planned for the big guns and mortars of his battle fleet to pound Fort McHenry into rubble. Then the British infantry would debark and storm the other fortifications around Baltimore.

Meanwhile, **Francis Scott Key** had sailed out to the British fleet under a flag of truce. Key, an American attorney, successfully negotiated an exchange of prisoners-of-war, including Dr. William Beanes, who was held captive aboard one of the British ships. The British agreed to release Beanes into the custody of Key *after* the coming battle, so Key remained at sea with the British fleet.

Shortly after noon on 13 September the British Navy opened fire. Safely beyond the range of Fort McHenry's guns, the British warships began blasting the American defenders. Sixteen lethal "bomb ships" fired huge 13-inch, 185-pound, high-explosive shells. Fired from over two miles away, these high-trajectory siege mortars began raining destruction down onto the Americans.

Waiting at sea and looking through his telescope, Key nervously watched the results of the bombardment. As nightfall approached, the symbol of American defiance -- the huge American flag with

15 stars and 15 stripes, approved by an act of Congress in 1794 -- was still visible "at the twilight's last gleaming." All through the night the shelling continued. In a night sky often illuminated by "the rockets' red glare, the bombs bursting in air," Key periodically could see the American flag atop the flagpole inside of Fort McHenry. Thus far, no capitulation!

Just before dawn the British guns and siege mortars fell silent. Had the fort surrendered? Had the American flag been hauled down? Soon aided "by the dawn's early light," Key peered through his telescope. He quickly spotted the flag of his country, still defiantly fluttering in the morning breeze. Elated and inspired, he began to compose a poem on the back of an envelope.

Thwarted, the British fleet sailed away, and Key headed back to Baltimore. In a hotel room he revised and edited his poem, and he titled it, *The Defense of Fort McHenry.* He then printed his new poem on handbills and circulated them throughout the city.

To celebrate the victory at Baltimore, the American public soon began singing the poem to the tune of a popular bar-room ballad, *To Anacreon in Heaven.* Its popularity grew, and the first official public performance took place the following month. The song gradually became known as *The Star Spangled Banner.*

Today "the star-spangled banner" that flew over Fort McHenry is preserved in the Smithsonian Museum in Washington, DC. By an act of Congress, *The Star Spangled Banner* became the National Anthem of the United States of America in 1931:

The Star Spangled Banner

O say, can you see, by the dawn's early light,
What so proudly we hail'd at the twilight's last gleaming?
Whose broad stripes and bright stars, thro' the perilous fight,
O'er the ramparts we watch'd, were so gallantly streaming?
And the rockets' red glare, the bombs bursting in air,
Gave proof thro' the night that our flag was still there.
O say, does that star-spangled banner yet wave,
O'er the land of the free and the home of the brave?

On the shore, dimly seen thro' the mists of the deep,
Where the foe's haughty host in dread silence reposes,

What is that which the breeze, o'er the towering steep,
As it fitfully blows, half conceals, half discloses?
Now it catches the gleam of the morning's first beam,
In full glory reflected, now shines on the stream:
'Tis the star-spangled banner! O, long may it wave,
O'er the land of the free and the home of the brave!

And where is that band who so vauntingly swore,
That the havoc of war and the battle's confusion,
A home and a country, shall leave us no more?
Their blood has wash'd out their foul footsteps' pollution.
No refuge could save the hireling and slave,
From the terror of flight or the gloom of the grave:
And the star-spangled banner in triumph doth wave,
O'er the land of the free and the home of the brave!

O, thus be it e'er when free men shall stand,
Between their lov'd homes and the war's desolation!
Blest with vict'ry and peace, may the heav'n-rescued land,
Praise the Pow'r that has made and preserv'd us a nation!
Then conquer we must when our cause is just,
And this be our motto: "In God is our trust!"
And the star-spangled banner in triumph shall wave,
O'er the land of the free and the home of the brave!

This flag of ours is the symbol of all that is good
about this country . . . Perhaps there are many
people in this nation who have never been abroad,
or in harm's way, and [who have] never seen the
flag upon their return. Those poor souls can never
know the deep pride and honor one feels to see it
wave, to know that there is still a good ol' USA.
With all our warts, we are still the greatest nation on
Earth, and the flag is the most powerful symbol of
that greatness.
    [Maj. Brian Schul, USAF, 3 October 2001]

Patriot Dreams

Patriot!   The word evokes thoughts of Paul Revere, Patrick Henry, and the American Revolution two-hundred-plus years ago. Yet, the meaning runs deeper than that.

Webster defines *patriot* as one "who loves, supports, and defends his country." By that definition our fledgling Republic had a host of patriots during the long-ago struggle for independence. Thomas Jefferson, George Washington, Nathan Hale, John Adams, Thomas Paine, and others gave us our "government of the people."

All of those men are now dead and gone.   Yet, a latter-day American Patriot reminds us that "Eternal vigilance is the price of freedom."   America's military warriors explain the same premise in different words: "The price of freedom is not cheap."

History has shown that foreign despots will always plague the world: Lenin, Hitler, Mao, Tito, Stalin, and their henchmen. Some barbarious tyrants like Tojo got the hangman's noose for their despicable deeds. Mussolini's countrymen went one better; they hung him *upside down.*

For others the ax has yet to fall.   Idi Amin, who fed his opponents to crocodiles, survived to live in exile with the millions he plundered.   Other tyrants still rule with an iron hand.   Of course, the United States is not immune.   Sometimes *our own* (Benedict Arnold, Bill Clinton, and their ilk) make a mockery of the trust vested in them.   Nonetheless, our society has persevered.

A one-of-a-kind American icon was born in Winterset, Iowa, in 1907.   His parents named him Marion Morrison, but the world would remember him as **John Wayne** (1907-1979). He embodied all that is virtuous and good about his native land.   He was a patriot, father, husband, humanitarian, actor, tycoon, role model, but most of all he was a genuine American hero.   He has been called an "extra star on the American Flag."   He *lived* the virtues that made him a legend.   Seventeen years after his death, a Harris Poll revealed that he is the most popular motion picture actor of all time.   John Wayne once explained his love for his country:

Sure I wave the American flag. Do you know of a better flag to wave? Sure I love my country with all her faults. I'm not ashamed of that. Never have been, never will be.

Fortunately each new generation has raised up American Patriots willing to sacrifice and serve. However, most of these modern-day patriots are not recognized as such. They are not like John Wayne. In our society, most of them are *invisible*.

The American Patriot of today is often the loyal legionnaire who dons his clothes with a prosthetic hand, without complaint. The patriot may be the stooped old man bagging groceries at the supermarket. Now palsied and slow, he never mentions the firestorm on Iwo Jima back in 1945, because he knows no one who could comprehend such indescribable horror. American Patriots also are the hundreds of thousands of forgotten warriors who went forth into battle for their country -- and who never returned.

Today's patriot is usually the common man, the average citizen, the next-door neighbor, the man who selflessly gave to his country and asked for nothing in return. The American Patriot of today may be a minimum wage laborer -- the same man who stormed into battle in Afghanistan in 2001 to restore freedom for people he would never know. Duty called. He answered.

Mao Tse-tung knew what he was talking about: "Power emanates from the barrel of a gun." Historically, after diplomacy and reason have failed our country always relies on its modern-day American Patriots, its military warriors.

Remember: when enemies and terrorists threaten, it is always the *warrior*, not the politician, who ensures the survival of our society. It is always the *warrior*, not the news media, who guarantees our freedom of the press. When the flak flies it is the *warrior*, not the lawyer, who preserves our civil liberties.

In March 2001 a twelfth grade schoolgirl in Ohio stumbled across a few vague paragraphs in her history textbook. Her country had fought a war in faraway Vietnam, she learned. Why? Who had fought? What was at stake? Although she had always been a history buff, the schoolgirl could not recall the name of any American involved in that conflict. Intrigued and challenged, she chose "Who Were The Heroes?" as the title of her senior thesis.

One warrior who fought in Vietnam answered the schoolgirl's

public query. He explained that the heroes were just ordinary men. Actually, *boys* would be a better description in most cases. But they were uniquely bound together. They shared a common bond, the schoolgirl was told. They believed in each other, and they believed in their cause. The warrior of yesteryear explained two instances wherein his friends had selflessly risked their lives to aid their brothers-in-arms in peril. Then he added:

> There were thousands of such heroes. Simply stated, they believed in a cause greater than themselves . . . The heroes who survived are now in their fifties or sixties. You know them as fathers, uncles, neighbors, maybe teachers. They have jobs and families. They pay taxes and make our society function. They don't label themselves as heroes. Yet, they are American Patriots in every sense of the words. And deep down inside they still maintain that undying brotherly love for the men with whom they served in Vietnam thirty years or so ago. Without question, they are your heroes.

Loyalty to brothers-in-arms, loyalty to cause, and patriotism! These virtues remain synonymous with the combat culture of all American military warriors. These virtues are inseparable; they are one. Loyalty and patriotism never go out of style. In every freedom loving nation, each generation has produced men who knew the meaning of service and sacrifice. We should pause and reflect on statements from them, and about them. These patriotic statements have been arranged in approximate chronological order:

Go tell the Spartans, thou that passeth by,
That here, obedient to the laws, we lie.
  [epitaph for the Spartan soldiers who fell in battle, holding the pass at Thermopylae in 480 BC]

Who here is so vile that will not love his country?
  [William Shakespeare (1564-1616), *Julius Caesar*]

Those who expect to reap the blessings of liberty must, like men, undergo the fatigue of supporting it.
  [Thomas Paine (1737-1809), American revolutionary author]

Is life so dear, or peace so sweet, as to be purchased at the price of chains and slavery? Forbid it, Almighty God! I know not what course others may take, but as for me, give me liberty, or give me death!
   [Patrick Henry, American colonial statesman; to the Virginia Convention of Delegates, 23 March 1775]

O ye that love mankind! Ye that dare oppose not only tyranny, but the tyrant, stand forth!
   [Thomas Paine, *Common Sense,* 1776]

. . . with a firm Reliance on the Protection of Divine Providence, we mutually pledge to each other our Lives, our Fortunes, and our sacred Honor.
   [Declaration of Independence, signed 4 July 1776]

Only a virtuous people are capable of freedom. *[and also]* Those who sacrifice essential liberty for temporary safety are not deserving of either liberty or safety.
   [Benjamin Franklin (1706-1790), American diplomat and author]

I only regret that I have but one life to lose for my country.
   [Capt. Nathan Hale, Continental Army; his last words before he was hanged as a spy by the British, 22 September 1776]

We fight, get beat, rise, and fight again.
   [MGen. Nathanael Greene, Continental Army; 22 June 1781]

The tree of liberty must be refreshed from time to time with the blood of patriots and tyrants.
   [Thomas Jefferson, American statesman; 13 November 1787]

You will never know how much it has cost my generation to preserve your freedom. I hope you will use it wisely.
   [John Adams (1735-1826), member of the Continental Congress, first U.S. Vice President, second U.S. President]

The only thing necessary for the triumph of evil is for good men

to do nothing.
  [Edmund Burke (1729-1797), British statesman]

In matters of principle, stand like a rock! *[and also]* I have
sworn, upon the altar of God, eternal hostility against every form
of tyranny over the mind of man.
  [Thomas Jefferson (1743-1826), U.S. President]

Breathes there a man with soul so dead,
Who never to himself hath said,
This is my own, my native land!
  [Sir Walter Scott, *Lay of the Last Minstrel*, 1805]

And the star spangled banner in triumph shall wave,
O'er the land of the free and the home of the brave.
  [Francis Scott Key, American attorney and prisoner exchange
  negotiator; *The Star Spangled Banner*, 14 September 1814 during
  the British bombardment of Fort McHenry (later adopted as the
  National Anthem of the United States on 3 March 1931)]

Our country! In her intercourse with foreign nations, may she
always be in the right. But, our country, right or wrong!
  [Commodore Stephen Decatur, USN; at Norfolk, Virginia, 1816]

To the People of Texas and all Americans in the world . . . I call
on you in the name of liberty, patriotism, & of everything dear in
the American character, to come to our aid with all dispatch.
  [LtCol. William B. Travis, Texas Volunteer Militia; at the Alamo
  in southwest Texas, 24 February 1836]

Let us fly to arms, march to the battlefield, meet the foe, and give
renewed evidence to the world that the arms of freemen, uplifted
in defense of liberty and right, are irresistible. Now is the day,
now is the hour, when Texas expects every man to do his duty.
Let us show ourselves worthy to be free, and we shall be free.
  [Henry Smith, Governor of Texas; 2 March 1836]

One country, one constitution, one destiny. *[and also]* I was born
an American; I live an American; I shall die an American. *[and*

also] God grants liberty to those who love it and are always ready to guard and defend it.
[Daniel Webster (1782-1852), U.S. Senator and orator]

America is great because she is good. If America ever ceases to be good, America will cease to be great.
[Alexis de Tocqueville (1805-1859), French historian]

If anyone attempts to haul down the American flag, shoot him on the spot.
[John A. Dix, U.S. Secretary of the Treasury; 1860]

All I am, and all I have, is at the service of my Country.
[LtGen. Thomas J. "Stonewall" Jackson, CSA; in a letter, 1861]

Fourscore and seven years ago our fathers brought forth on this continent a new nation, conceived in liberty, and dedicated to the proposition that all men are created equal.
[Abraham Lincoln, U.S. President; at the dedication of the National Cemetery at Gettysburg battlefield, 19 November 1863]

Dear Madam: I have been shown in the files of the War Department a statement of the Adjutant General of Massachusetts [which shows] that you are the mother of five sons who have died gloriously on the field of battle. I feel how weak and fruitless must be any words of mine which should attempt to beguile you from the grief of a loss so overwhelming. But I cannot refrain from tendering you the consolation that may be found in the thanks of the Republic they died to save. I pray that our heavenly Father may assuage the anguish of your bereavement, and leave you only the cherished memory of the loved and lost, and the solemn pride that must be yours to have laid so costly a sacrifice upon the altar of freedom.
[Abraham Lincoln, U.S. President; in a letter to Mrs. Lydia Bixbey, 21 November 1864 (read verbatim 134 years later in the motion picture, *Saving Private Ryan*, 1998)]

The muster rolls on which the name and oath were written were pledges of honor -- redeemable at the gates of death. And those

who went up to them, knowing this, are on the list of heroes.
[BGen. Joshua L. Chamberlain, USA; writing of the Union and Confederate volunteers during the American Civil War, 1866]

War is an ugly thing, but not the ugliest thing. The decayed and degraded state of moral and patriotic feelings which thinks that nothing is worse than war is much worse. A man who has nothing for which he is willing to fight, nothing which is more important than his own personal safety, is a miserable creature and has no chance of being free -- unless made and kept so by the exertions of better men than himself.
[John S. Mill, British philosopher; 1868]

There is something magnificent about having a country to love.
[James Russell Lowell (1819-1891), American poet]

Eternal vigilance is the price of liberty.
[Wendell Phillips (1811-1884), American orator]

A thoughtful mind, when it sees a Nation's flag, sees not the flag only, but the Nation itself.
[Henry Ward Beecher (1813-1887), American philosopher]

A man's country is not a certain area of land . . . it is a principle; and patriotism is loyalty to that principle.
[George William Curtis (1824-1892), American author]

I pledge allegiance to the Flag of the United States of America and to the Republic for which it stands, one nation, under God, indivisible, with liberty and justice for all.
[Francis R. Bellamy, Baptist minister; *Pledge to the Flag*, 1892 (the words "under God" were subsequently added)]

O beautiful for Heroes proved, in liberating strife,
Who more than self their country loved, and mercy more than life!
America! America! May God thy gold refine,
Till all success be nobleness, and every gain divine.
O beautiful for Patriot Dream, that sees beyond the years,
Thine alabaster cities gleam, undimmed by human tears!

America! America! God shed His grace on thee,
And crown thy good with brotherhood, from sea to shining sea.
  [Katherine L. Bates, excerpt from *America the Beautiful*, 1893]

Liberty means responsibilities.
  [George Bernard Shaw (1856-1950), Irish philosopher]

Our flag is our national ensign, pure and simple, behold it! Listen
to it! Every star has a tongue, every stripe is articulate.
  [Robert C. Winthrop (1809-1894), U.S. Senator]

My country, 'tis of thee, sweet land of liberty,
Of thee I sing; land where my fathers died,
Land of the pilgrims' pride, from every mountainside,
Let freedom ring!
  [Samuel F. Smith (1808-1895), *My Country, 'Tis of Thee*]

Order without liberty, and liberty without order, are equally
destructive.
  [Col. Theodore Roosevelt (1858-1919), USA; U.S. President]

. . . I therefore believe it is my duty to my country to love it, to
support its Constitution, to obey its laws, to respect its flag, and to
defend it against all enemies.
  [William Tyler Page, *The American Creed*, 1917]

The meaning of America is not a life without toil. Freedom is not
only bought with a great price, it is maintained by unremitting
effort. *[and also]* Patriotism is easy to understand in America. It
means looking out for yourself by looking out for your country.
  [Calvin Coolidge (1872-1933), U.S. President]

The only thing we have to fear is fear itself.
  [Franklin D. Roosevelt, U.S. President; 4 March 1933]

One flag, one land, one heart, one hand, one nation, evermore.
  [Oliver Wendell Holmes Jr. (1841-1935), American jurist]

It is the love of country that has lighted, and that keeps glowing,

the holy fire of patriotism.
  [J. Horace McFarland (1859-1948), political observer]

We shall fight on the beaches. We shall fight in the landing
grounds. We shall fight in the fields and in the streets. We shall
fight in the hills. We shall never surrender.
  [Sir Winston Churchill, British Prime Minister; speaking in the
  House of Commons, 4 June 1940, after Dunkirk]

Only our individual faith in freedom can keep us free.
  [Gen. Dwight D. Eisenhower, USA; also U.S. President, 1952]

Patriotism is not short frenzied outbursts of emotion, but the
tranquil and steady dedication of a lifetime.
  [Adlai E. Stevensen (1900-1965), American diplomat]

Live free or die.
  [motto of the State of New Hampshire]

I am an American, fighting in the armed forces which guard my
country and our way of life. I am prepared to give my life in their
defense.
  [Article I, Code of Conduct; U.S. Armed Forces, 1955]

Let every nation know, whether it wishes us well or ill, that we
shall pay any price, bear any burden, meet any hardship, support
any friend, oppose any foe, to assure the survival and success of
liberty. *[and also]* Ask not what your country can do for you.
Ask what you can do for your country.
  [John F. Kennedy, U.S. President; 20 January 1961]

The last time any of his fellow prisoners heard from him, Captain
Versace was singing *God Bless America* at the top of his voice.
  [from Medal of Honor citation, Capt. Humbert Roque "Rocky"
  Versace, USA; a POW who was dragged from a bamboo cage
  and executed by the enemy on 26 September 1965]

. . . he sustained multiple fragmentation wounds from exploding
grenades as he ran to an abandoned machine gun position . . .

Corporal Maxam's position received a direct hit from a rocket propelled grenade, knocking him backwards and inflicting severe fragmentation wounds to his face and right eye. Although momentarily stunned and in intense pain, Corporal Maxam courageously resumed his firing position and subsequently was struck again by small arms fire . . . the [enemy] threw hand grenades and directed recoilless rifle fire against him, inflicting two additional wounds. Too weak to reload his machine gun, Corporal Maxam fell to a prone position and valiantly continued to deliver effective fire with his rifle. After one and a half hours, during which he was hit repeatedly by fragments from exploding grenades and concentrated small arms fire, he succumbed to his wounds . .
  He gallantly gave his life for his country.
  [Medal of Honor citation, Cpl. Larry L. Maxam, USMC; 1968]

He insisted on giving his life so that forty of his fellow Marines might live and triumph. He had freely chosen loyalty above life.
  [1stLt. Michael Stick, USMC; speaking of Cpl. Larry L. Maxam, USMC, killed-in-action in Vietnam, 2 February 1968]

We are **honored** to have had the **opportunity** to serve our country under difficult circumstances. We are profoundly **grateful** to our Commander-and-Chief and to our Nation for this day. **God bless America!**
  [Capt. Jeremiah A. Denton Jr., USN; former POW in North Vietnam for eight years, upon his release on 13 February 1973]

America is a passionate idea . . . America is a human brotherhood.
  [Max Lerner (1902-1992), political commentator]

Let the Fourth of July always be a reminder that here in this land, for the first time, it was decided that man is born with certain God-given rights; that government is only a convenience created and managed by the people, with no power of its own except those voluntarily granted to it by the people. We sometimes forget that great truth, and we never should.
  [Ronald Reagan, U.S. President; 4 July 1981]

It is my heritage to stand erect, proud and unafraid. To think and

act for myself, enjoy the benefit of my creations; to face the whole world and boldly say, "I am a free American."
[excerpt from *The Republican Creed*]

Sure, war is hell. But some things are worse than hell -- slavery being one.
[RAdm. Jeremiah A. Denton Jr., USN; U.S. Senator, reflecting upon his eight years as a POW in North Vietnam]

The Marines knew they were fighting for freedom, and they had an enormous respect for basic American values.
[SSgt. Arvin S. Gibson, USA; *In Search of Angels*, 1990]

You can just call me an American Patriot.
[Maj. Harry R. "Bob" Mills, USMC; to a friend, 1991]

I swore to defend my nation against all enemies, foreign and domestic. It doesn't get any simpler. Stop trying to understand us.
[unidentified corporal, in *A Sense of Values*, 1994]

The red, white, and blue flag of the United States of America triumphantly fluttered in the stiff breeze atop Hill 881 North, deep in the heart of Indochina.
[Capt. Marion F. Sturkey, USMC; *Bonnie-Sue*, 1996]

The price of freedom is not cheap.
[*Guidebook for Marines*, Marine Corps Association, 1997]

I gave more to America than I ever took from America, and I am proud of it. Semper Fi! And, God bless you all.
[Col. Wayne Shaw, USMC; upon his retirement from the Corps]

America's freedom, and the values that protect us in the face of evil, are our great and glorious cause.
[RAdm. John McCain, USN; also U.S. Senator, September 2001]

Semper Fi, brothers! God bless the United States and the Corps!
[2ndLt. John E. Fales, USMC; 12 September 2001]

This will be a battle between good and evil . . . It will be an honor to fight for God, country, and the good of mankind.
  [LCpl. Thomas C. Macedo, USMC; 20 September 2001]

There will never be another nation such as ours. Take good care of her. The fate of the world depends upon it.
  [RAdm. John McCain, USN; also U.S. Senator, at the U.S. Naval Academy, 9 October 2001]

God has blessed America with much bounty and many fine men and women through the years, who have risked their lives -- then given them -- to preserve our liberty.
  [Dr. David Russell, American Legion chaplain; 18 October 2001]

Vocal patriotism is a form of protest against terrorism.
  [C. Welton Gaddy, in *Liberty*, 2002]

I do solemnly swear, or affirm, that I will support and defend the Constitution of the United States against all enemies, foreign and domestic; that I will bear true faith and allegiance to the same; that I will obey the orders of the President of the United States and the orders of the officers appointed over me, according to regulations and the Uniform Code of Military Justice. So help me God.
  [Oath of Enlistment, United States Armed Forces]

****

Note: A list of American patriotic statements should include the lyrics of the song, *God Bless America*, and the lyrics of the refrain from the song, *God Bless the USA*.

Irving Berlin wrote *God Bless America* in 1938, based upon similar lyrics he had composed in 1918. Kate Smith popularized the song by introducing it and singing it on her radio broadcast on Armistice Day (now, Veterans Day) later that year. Rights to the lyrics are held by a third party.

The more recent *God Bless the USA* was popularized by Lee Greenwood. Rights to the lyrics are held by a third party.

Combat Axioms
for
American Warriors

The Profession of Arms! Since time immemorial the professional warrior has always been a key player on the world stage.

Non-combatants look at warriors and see either honor and glory, or horror and hardship. Yet, down through the centuries the professional warrior has not concerned himself with what non-combatants see or believe. Instead, the warrior has only three immediate concerns: (1) loyalty to brothers-in-arms, (2) allegiance to cause, and (3) success in battle -- often called *staying alive* in battle. A true professional warrior possesses all three of these concerns. One or two will not suffice.

Success in battle, like success in any other human endeavor, hinges on proven principles. These basic principles do not change. Weapons change. Technology changes. Nations rise, nations fall. Causes come, causes go. Yet, the basic principles, or axioms, of warfare remain constant.

Below are selected jewels of wisdom and advice which will benefit the professional warrior. Most of these statements come from warriors who have tasted the sting of battle. Others come from authors, philosophers, and heads of state. These are **fighting words for fighting men**. Readers will find no sensitivity session childishness. No edicts from bean counters. Nothing from REMFs or paper-pushers, no logistics theories. No admonitions about social etiquette or liberal feminist tomfoolery. No administrative orders from staff pogues or library assistants. Instead, these are **combat axioms**, a unique collection for American Warriors. For continuity these axioms are displayed chronologically. Professional warriors of today: read, heed, and persevere in battle:

Our business in the field of fight
Is not to question, but to fight.
[Homer, *The Iliad*, c 800 BC]

All warfare is based on deception. *[and also]* Invincibility lies in the defense; the possibility of victory in the attack. One defends when his strength is inadequate; he attacks when it is abundant.
   [Sun Tzu, *The Art of War*, c 500 BC]

Great deeds are usually wrought at great risk.
   [Herodotus (c 490-425 BC), Greek historian]

Danger gleams like sunshine to a brave man's eyes. *[and also]* There is nothing like the sight of an enemy down on his luck.
   [Euripides (c 485-406 BC), Greek poet and playwright]

The bravest are surely those who have the clearest vision of what is before them, glory and danger alike, and yet notwithstanding, go out to meet it.
   [Thucydides (460-400 BC), Greek historian]

The Spartans do not ask how many the enemy number, but where they are.
   [Ages of Sparta, venerated Spartan sage, c 415 BC]

In war, opportunity waits for no man.
   [Pericles, Athenian statesman; *The Peloponnesian War,* 404 BC]

Stand firm, for well you know that hardship and danger are the price of glory!
   [Alexander the Great (356-323 BC), during a battle in India]

The greater the difficulty, the greater the glory.
   [Cicero (c 106-43 BC), Roman Consul and orator]

I came. I saw. I conquered.
   [Julius Caesar, Roman General; the entire text of his dispatch to the Roman Senate after his victory at the Battle of Zela, 47 BC]

Let them hate us as long as they fear us.
   [Caligula (c 12-41 AD), Roman Emperor]

The body of a dead enemy always smells sweet.
  [Aulus Vitellius, Roman Emperor; at Beariacum, 69 AD]

Let him who desires peace prepare for war.
  [Vegetius, Roman military strategist; c 400 AD]

The greatest happiness is to vanquish your enemies.
  [Genghis Khan (1162-1227), Mongol conqueror]

The infantry must ever be regarded as the very foundation and nerve of an army.
  [Niccolo Machiavelli (1469-1527), *Discourses*]

It is fighting at a great disadvantage to fight those who have nothing to lose.
  [Francesco Guiciardini, *Storia d'Italia*, 1564]

Cowards die many times before their deaths;
The valiant never taste of death but once.
  [William Shakespeare (1564-1616), *Julius Caesar*]

We few, we happy few, we band of brothers;
For he today that sheds his blood with me
Shall be my brother.
  [William Shakespeare (1564-1616), *Henry V*]

A man-o-war is the best ambassador.
  [Oliver Cromwell (1599-1658), Lord Protector of Ireland]

The first blow is half the battle.
  [Oliver Goldsmith, British novelist; *She Stoops to Conquer*, 1773]

Battles are won by superiority of fire. *[and also]* He who tries to defend everything defends nothing.
  [Frederick the Great (1712-1786), *Military Testament*]

The battle, sir, is not to the strong alone. It is to the vigilant, the active, the brave.
  [Patrick Henry, American statesman; addressing the Virginia

Convention of Delegates, 23 March 1775]

We must all hang together, or, we shall all hang separately.
[Benjamin Franklin, American statesman; after signing the Declaration of Independence, 4 July 1776]

If we desire to avoid insult, we must be able to repel it. If we desire peace, it must be known that we are ready for war.
[Gen. George Washington (1732-1799), Continental Army]

Let us beware of being lulled into a dangerous security of being weakened by internal contentions and diversions; of neglect in military exercises and disciplines in providing stores and arms and munitions of war.
[Benjamin Franklin (1706-1790), American statesman]

March to the sound of the guns.
[the Duke of York, British noble; 1793]

No military leader has ever become great without audacity.
[MGen. Carl von Clausewitz, strategist; *Principles of War*, 1812]

Don't give up the ship! Fight her until she sinks!
[Capt. James Lawrence, USN; mortally wounded aboard his frigate, *USS Chesapeake*, 1 June 1813]

One man with courage is a majority.
[Thomas Jefferson (1743-1826), U.S. President]

Glory may be fleeting, but obscurity is forever. *[and also]* Moral forces, rather than numbers, decide victory. *[and also]* Good infantry is, without doubt, the sinew of an army. *[and also]* Never interrupt your enemy when he is making a mistake. *[and also]* The bayonet has always been the weapon of the brave and the chief tool of victory. *[and also]* Four hostile newspapers are more to be feared than a thousand bayonets.
[Napoleon Bonaparte, Emperor of France, charismatic military warrior and tactician; *Maxims of War*, 1831]

The best strategy is always to be strong. *[and also]* Blood is the price of victory.
  [MGen. Carl von Clausewitz, strategist; *On War*, 1832]

Our flag still waves proudly from the walls . . . I shall never surrender nor retreat . . . I am determined to sustain myself as long as possible and die like a soldier who never forgets what is due to his own honor and that of his country. Victory or Death!
  [LtCol. William B. Travis, Texas Volunteer Militia; in his last dispatch from the Alamo, 24 February 1836]

Gone to Florida to fight the Indians. Will be back when the war is over.
  [Col. Archibald Henderson, USMC, Marine Corps Commandant; in a handwritten note glued to his office door, 1836]

A great country can not wage a little war.
  [Duke of Wellington; in the House of Lords, 16 January 1838]

We should forgive our enemies -- but *only* after they have been hanged first.
  [Heinrich Heine (1797-1856), German philosopher]

I was too weak to defend, so I attacked. *[and also]* Do your duty in all things. You can not do more. You should never do less.
  [Gen. Robert E. Lee (1807-1870), CSA]

There is a true glory and a true honor -- the glory of duty done, the honor of the integrity of principle.
  [Gen. Robert E. Lee, CSA; in *Southern Historical Society Papers*]

Get 'em skeered, and keep the skeer on 'em. *[and also]* I always make it a rule to get there first'est with the most'est. *[and also]* In any fight, it's the first blow that counts the most. *[and also]* War is fighting, and fighting means killing.
  [LtGen. Nathan Bedford Forrest (1821-1877), CSA]

I make no terms. I accept no compromises.
  [Jefferson Davis (1808-1889), C.S.A. President]

There! There! There is Jackson! Standing like a stone wall!
[the rallying shout of an unidentified CSA officer at the battle of
Bull Run (also called, First Manassas) on 21 July 1861, referring
to BGen. Thomas J. "Stonewall" Jackson, CSA]

Success and glory are in the advance. Disaster and shame lurk in
the rear.
[MGen. John Pope, USA; in a General Order, 14 July 1862]

Always mystify, mislead, and surprise the enemy. *[and also]*
Duty is ours, consequences are God's. *[and also]* What is life
without honor? Degradation is worse than death! *[and also]* An
enemy routed, if hotly pursued, becomes panic-stricken and can be
destroyed by half their number. *[and also]* To move swiftly,
strike vigorously, and secure the fruits of victory is the secret of
successful war. *[and also]* The business of the soldier is to fight,
to find the enemy and strike him, invade his country, and do him
all possible damage in the shortest possible time.
[LtGen. Thomas J. "Stonewall" Jackson (1824-1863), CSA]

My religious belief teaches me to feel as safe in battle as in bed.
[LtGen. Thomas J. "Stonewall" Jackson, CSA; quoted years later,
posthumously, in *Stonewall Jackson*, 1898]

We will fight them until Hell freezes over, and then we will fight
them on the ice.
[unidentified Confederate Army soldier, Gettysburg, 3 July 1863]

We must substitute *esprit* for numbers.
[MGen. J.E.B. "Jeb" Stuart (1833-1864), CSA]

Get your enemy at a disadvantage and never, on any account, fight
him on equal terms.
[George Bernard Shaw, British author; *Arms and the Man*, 1894]

Civilize 'em with a Krag.
[motto of the U.S. Marines in China during the Boxer Rebellion
in 1900, in regard to their Krag-Jorgensen rifles]

Courage is resistance to fear, mastery of fear, not absence of fear.
[Samuel L. Clemens (1835-1910), a.k.a. Mark Twain]

Speak softly, and carry a big stick.
[Col. Theodore "Teddy" Roosevelt, USA; U.S. Vice President, 2 September 1901]

I want no prisoners. I wish you to burn and kill. The more you burn and kill, the better it will please me.
[BGen. Jacob H. Smith, USA; in his order to Maj. L.W.T. Waller, in Samar, October 1901]

A man who is good enough to shed his blood for his Country is good enough to be given a square deal afterwards.
[Col. Theodore "Teddy" Roosevelt, USA; U.S. President, 1903]

Those who cannot remember the past are condemned to repeat it.
[George Santayana, philosopher; *A Life of Reason*, 1906]

The essence of war is violence. Moderation in war is imbecility.
[Adm. Sir John Fisher, RN; in a letter, 25 April 1912]

Find the enemy and shoot him down. Anything else is nonsense. *[and also]* The aggressive spirit, the offensive, is the chief thing everywhere in war, and the air is no exception.
[Baron Capt. Manfred von Richthofen, German Flying Service ("The Red Baron" of Germany, 80 air-to-air kills, WW I); 1917]

A pacifist is as surely a traitor to his country and to humanity as is the most brutal wrongdoer.
[Col. Theodore "Teddy" Roosevelt, USA; former U.S. President, 27 July 1917]

Retreat, Hell! We just got here!
[Capt. Lloyd Williams, USMC; to the retreating French Army commander who pleaded with him to flee from the attacking German Army in Belleau Wood, France, 2 June 1918]

Come on, you sons of bitches! Do you want to live forever?
[GySgt. Daniel J. "Dan" Daly, USMC; as he led the attack into
Belleau Wood near Lucy 'le Bocage, France, 6 June 1918]

The will to conquer is the first condition of victory.
[Marsh. Ferdinand Foch, French Army; *Principles of War*, 1920]

War hath no fury like a noncombatant.
[Charles E. Montague, *Disenchantment*, 1922]

To be vanquished and yet not surrender, that is victory.
[Marsh. Josef Pilsudski (1867-1935), Polish Army]

The advantage of sea power used offensively is that, when a fleet
sails, one can never be sure where it is going to strike.
[Sir Winston Churchill, *Their Finest Hour*, 1924]

People sleep peaceably in their beds at night only because rough
men stand ready to do violence on their behalf.
[George Orwell (1903-1950), novelist and philosopher]

Through mobility we conquer.
[motto of The Cavalry School, USA; Fort Riley, c 1930]

To wound all ten fingers of a man is not so effective as to chop
one of them off. To rout ten of the enemy's divisions is not so
effective as to annihilate one of them.
[Mao Tse-tung, Chairman of the People's Republic of China and
Commander-in-Chief of the Army; December 1936]

Power emanates from the barrel of a gun.
[Mao Tse-tung, Chairman of the People's Republic of China and
Commander-in-Chief of the Army; *On Guerrilla War*, 1938]

The more we sweat in peace, the less we bleed in war.
[Vijaya L. Pandit (1900-1990), Indian diplomat]

We are so outnumbered there's only one thing to do -- attack!
[Sir Andrew Cunningham, RN; at Taranto, 11 November 1940]

Sure I am of this. You have to endure to conquer. *[and also]*
The only thing you must really do is never, never, never, give up.
[and also] Nothing is worse than war? Dishonor is worse than
war. Slavery is worse than war. *[and also]* Battles are won by
slaughter and manoeuver.
   [Sir Winston Churchill (1874-1965), Prime Minister of Britain]

Victory at all costs, victory in spite of all terror, victory however
long and hard the road may be; for without victory there is no
survival.
   [Sir Winston Churchill; in the House of Commons, 13 May 1940]

Praise the Lord, and pass the ammunition!
   [Lt. Howell M. Forgy, USN chaplain; to the Navy antiaircraft
   gun crews aboard the *USS New Orleans* during the Japanese air
   attack at Pearl Harbor, Hawaii, 7 December 1941]

Put your heart and soul into being an expert killer. The only good
enemy is a dead enemy.
   [Gen. George S. Patton Jr., USA (who was perhaps paraphrasing
   Gen. Philip H. Sheridan, USA, who stated c 1868, "The only
   good Indian is a dead Indian."); March 1942]

God favors the bold and the strong of heart.
   [MGen. Alexander A. Vandergriff, USMC; August 1942]

A pint of sweat will save a gallon of blood.
   [Gen. George S. Patton Jr., USA; 8 November 1942]

You'll never get a Purple Heart hiding in a foxhole! Follow me!
   [Capt. Henry P. Crowe, USMC; Guadalcanal, 13 January 1943]

Before we're through with them, the Japanese language will be
spoken only in Hell.
   [Adm. William F. "Bull" Halsey, USN; 1943]

Casualties many, percentage of dead not known, combat efficiency:
we are winning.
   [Col. David M. Shoup, USMC; Tarawa, 21 November 1943]

Nobody ever won a war by dying for his country. You win a war by making the *other* poor dumb bastard die for *his* country. *[and also]* We don't want yellow cowards in this Army. They should be killed off like rats. *[and also]* War is a bloody, killing business. You've got to spill their blood, or they will spill yours. Rip them up the belly! Shoot them in the guts!
  [Gen. George S. Patton Jr., USA; addressing the soldiers of his Third Army, in England, 5 June 1944]

Lead me, follow me, or get out of my way!
  [Gen. George S. Patton Jr. (1885-1945), USA]

Wars may be fought with weapons, but they are won by men.
  [Gen. George S. Patton Jr., USA; in *The Cavalry Journal*]

Hurry up and whip these Germans so we can get out to the Pacific to kick the [expletive] out of the [expletive] Japanese.
  [Gen. George S. Patton Jr., USA; to his soldiers, spring 1945]

We're not accustomed to occupying defensive positions. It's destructive to morale.
  [LtGen. Holland "Howlin' Mad" Smith, USMC; Iwo Jima, 1945]

No sane man is unafraid in battle. But discipline produces in him a form of vicarious courage. *[and also]* To halt under fire is *folly*. To halt under fire, and not fire back, is *suicide*.
  [Gen. George S. Patton Jr., USA; quoted posthumously in *War as I Knew It*, 1947]

Darkness is a friend to the skilled infantryman. *[and also]* In war the chief incalculable is the human will.
  [Sir B.H. Liddell Hart, British Army; *Thoughts on War*, 1944]

See; Decide; Attack; Reverse.
  [Col. Erich Hartmann, Luftwaffe; 352 air-to-air kills, WW II]

In war there is no second prize for the runner-up.
  [Gen. Omar Bradley, USA; in *Military Review*, February 1950]

Those poor bastards. They've got us surrounded. Good! Now we can fire in any direction. They won't get away this time! *[and also]* Don't forget that you're First Marines! Not all the communists in Hell can overrun you!
[Col. Lewis B. "Chesty" Puller, USMC; when told that his regiment was surrounded by seven Chinese Divisions near the Chosin Reservoir in Korea, December 1950]

Hit quickly, hit hard, and keep on hitting.
[LtGen. Holland M. "Howlin' Mad" Smith, USMC; *Coral and Brass*, 1949]

Give me an order to do it. I can break up Russia's five A-bomb nests in a week. And when I go up to meet Christ, I think I could explain to Him that I had saved civilization.
[MGen. Orvil A. Anderson, USAF; 1950]

It is fatal to enter any war without the will to win it.
[Gen. Douglas MacArthur, USA; 7 July 1952]

War is never prevented by running away from it.
[Air Marsh. Sir John Slessor, RAF; *Strategy for the West*, 1954]

Diplomacy has rarely been able to gain at the conference table what cannot be gained or held on the battlefield.
[Gen. Walter B. Smith, USA; on his return from the Geneva Conference on Korea and Indochina, 1954]

Success in battle. That is the only objective of military training.
[LtGen. Lewis B. "Chesty" Puller, USMC; 2 August 1956]

Diplomacy is the art of saying "Nice doggie" until you can find a bigger rock.
[Wynn Catlin, Texas political observer]

It is essential to understand that battles are won primarily in the hearts of men.
[Viscount Field Marsh. Montgomery, British Army; *The Memoirs of Field Marshall Montgomery*, 1958]

There is nothing like seeing the other fellow run to bring back your courage.
  [Sir William Slim, British Army; *Unofficial History*, 1959]

In war there is no substitute for victory. *[and also]* Duty, Honor, Country. These three hallowed words reverently dictate what you ought to be, what you can be, what you will be.
  [Gen. Douglas MacArthur, USA; at West Point, 12 May 1962]

Appeasers believe that if you keep on throwing steaks to a tiger, the tiger will become a vegetarian.
  [Heywood Brown, American novelist]

Glory is not an end in itself, but rather a reward for valor and faith.
  [William J. Bennett, American political observer and educator]

Get the blade into the enemy. This is the main principle in bayonet fighting. It is the blade that kills.
  [*Guidebook for Marines*, Marine Corps Association, 1962]

Victory is always possible for the person who refuses to stop fighting.
  [Napoleon Hill, motivational writer]

Do not fear the enemy, for, at the worst, he can only take your life. Instead, a wise warrior fears **the media**, for he knows the sniveling media whores may steal his honor.
  [SSgt. Robert Johnson, USA; responding to a question from a high school student who had asked about a soldier's greatest fear in combat, in Fort Worth, Texas, August 2001]

The fundamental law of wartime negotiations: you negotiate with the enemy with your knee in his chest and your knife at his throat.
  [Gary J. Harris, military theorist]

I have always regarded the forward edge of the battlefield as the most exclusive club in the world.
  [LtGen. Sir Brian Horrocks, British Army; *A Full Life*, 1960]

It isn't the size of the dog in the fight that counts. It's the size of the fight in the dog.
[Gen. Dwight D. Eisenhower (1890-1969), USA; U.S. President]

Find, fix, fight, follow, finish.
[universal military axiom for *destroying* the enemy]

If your bayonet breaks, strike with the stock. If the stock gives way, hit with your fists. If your fists are hurt, bite with your teeth.
[Gen. Makhail Dragomirov, Russian Army; *Notes for Soldiers*]

.30 cals. won't hurt you if your mind's right.
[sign in the helicopter pilots' ready room tent, Vietnam, 1967]

Answer violence with violence!
[Col. Juan D. Peron (1895-1974), President of Argentina]

The only men fit to live are those men who are not afraid to die.
[motto of USN/USMC carrier-qualification training squadron VT-5; Pensacola, Florida]

Marines defending are like Antichrists at vespers.
[Michael Herr, *Dispatches*, 1968]

If you're in a fair fight, you didn't plan it properly.
[Nick Lappos, Chief R&D pilot, Sikorsky Aircraft Corp.]

A battle plan is good only until enemy contact is made.
[Gen. H. Norman Schwarzkopf, USA; 1988]

Fight to fly, Fly to fight, Fight to win.
[motto of USN/USMC Fighter Weapons (Top Gun) School]

We should negotiate only when our military superiority is so convincing that we can achieve our objectives at the conference table, and deny the aggressor theirs. *[and also]* The finest steel has gone through the hottest fire.
[Richard M. Nixon (1913-1994), U.S. President]

If you don't fight, you can't win. No guts, no glory.
  [anonymous]

A Marine's most sought after privilege is to be able to fight for another Marine.
  [MGen. Mike Myatt, USMC; Kuwait, 1991]

I love the Corps for those intangible possessions that cannot be issued: pride, honor, integrity, and being able to carry on the traditions for generations of warriors past.
  [Cpl. Jeff Sornig, USMC; in *Navy Times*, November 1994]

We fought for each other, or to uphold the honor of the Corps. That was what mattered.
  [Capt. Angus Deming, USMC; in *Newsweek*, 7 August 1995]

We might succeed, or we might fail, but we would succeed or fail together. There was no other Marine Corps way.
  [Capt. Marion F. Sturkey, USMC; *Bonnie-Sue*, 1996]

The purpose of offensive combat is to destroy the enemy and his will to fight.
  [*Guidebook for Marines*, Marine Corps Association, 1997]

Nothing in life is more liberating than to fight for a cause larger than yourself.
  [RAdm. John McCain, USN; former POW in North Vietnam, later a U.S. Senator, *Faith of My Fathers*, 1999]

When America uses force in the world, the cause must be just, the goal must be clear, and the victory must be overwhelming.
  [George W. Bush, presidential candidate (later U.S. President); addressing the Republican National Convention, 4 August 2000]

At the tip of the spear, there is no room for second best.
  [Bell Helicopter Public Affairs, September 2000]

When you are in the military and at war, there is no such thing as

innocence. It's called kill or be killed.
  [MGen. J.J. Johnson, USMC; 19 July 2001]

They should be caught, drawn & quartered, decapitated, and their
ugly [expletive] heads put on pikes in front of the White House.
  [Maj. Bill F. Weaver, USMC; 12 September 2001]

I say to our enemies, God may show you mercy. We will not.
  [RAdm. John McCain, USN; also U.S. Senator, addressing the
  U.S. Senate, 12 September 2001]

I don't care what God they believe in, but they better get close to
him, 'cause they are about to meet him face to face.
  [Sgt. Robert J. "Bob" Kowalk, USMC; 13 September 2001]

  Let the enemy know the full fury of an America that
  has been wronged and demands retribution. Kill
  them all!
    [Sgt. Arthur W. Larsen, USMC; writing to his
    friends on 13 September 2001]

The Blood Chit
and
Air America

-- The Blood Chit --

The blood chit is the document that America's aerial warriors always want to have, but never want to use.

Blood chit is the common term for the written notice, in several languages, carried by American military aircrews in combat. If their aircraft is shot down, the notice identifies the warriors as Americans and encourages the local population to assist them.

The concept is over 200 years old. Jean-Pierre Blanchard, the famous French balloonist, came to America in 1793 to demonstrate hot air balloon flight. He would ascend from Philadelphia. Where he would come down, of course, no one knew. Further, Blanchard did not speak English. George Washington, the U.S. President, gave Blanchard a letter addressed to "All citizens of the United States." The letter asked that Blanchard be befriended and given safe passage back to Philadelphia.

Thereafter this idea lay dormant for over 100 years. But in World War I the British RAF issued "ransom notes" to its combat pilots flying in India and Mesopotamia. These notes, written in Arabic, Urdu, Farsi, and Pashto languages, promised a reward to anyone bringing an "unharmed" British pilot or observer to the nearest British outpost. British airmen called the notes "goolie chits" (goolie was the Hindustani word for *ball*). Many hostile tribesmen had been turning captured airmen over to local women for *castration*, so ransom notes included the word, unharmed.

When the mercenary Flying Tigers went to China in 1937 to battle the Japanese, they carried "blood chits." These printed notices bore the Chinese flag and Chinese lettering which stated:

This foreign person has come to China to help in the war effort.

Soldiers and civilians, one and all, should rescue, protect, and provide him with medical care.

Later when the United States officially entered the war in 1941, it issued blood chits in almost 50 different languages. A reward was offered to those who assisted downed fliers.

The U.S. government kept its word. The greatest reward ever given went to the family that aided a B-29 crew shot down on 12 July 1950, two weeks after the start of the Korean War. North Korean civilians found the badly injured American crewmen. Yu Ho Chun discovered the blood chit in the pocket of one flier. He gave the Americans medical aid. Then, at great personal risk, he put them on a junk and sailed them 100 miles down the coast to safety. Two weeks later the North Korean Army found Chun, tortured him, and then killed him. But 43 years later in 1993 the United States paid a $100,000.00 reward to his son, Yu Song Dan.

During the war in Vietnam the fighter, attack, and helicopter crews carried updated blood chits. These chits displayed the American flag, plus an appeal in 14 languages: English, Burmese, Thai, Old Chinese, New Chinese, Laotian, Cambodian, Tagalog, Vietnamese, Visayan, Malayan, French, Indonesian, and Dutch. The translation in each language was the same:

I am a citizen of the United States of America. I do not speak your language. Misfortune forces me to seek your assistance in obtaining food, shelter, and protection. Please take me to someone who will provide for my safety and see that I am returned to my people. My government will reward you.

In Vietnam, as in World War II, some unique missions required unique measures. On certain *Black Ops* flights, in addition to their blood chits, the aircrews carried paper money and gold coins. Needless to say, these required strict inventory control. Upon return from a mission, "I lost the money!" would not suffice.

Today the United States has pre-printed blood chits for most locations throughout the world. Blood chits in the appropriate languages were issued to American aerial warriors for operations in Panama, Grenada, Somalia, Bosnia, Afghanistan, Iraq, and other hot-spots around the globe. Since the beginning of the new millennium in the year 2000, America's military aircrews have continued to carry blood chits while flying in combat in Southwest Asia and elsewhere. In the ongoing battle against international terrorism, the blood chit package often includes money, and sometimes a pointee-talkee pictorial display.

-- Air America --

Any gung-ho American Warrior knows, or has heard, *something* about Air America. Maybe he has read the well-documented book. It was first published in Great Britain in 1979 under the title, *The Invisible Air Force: The True Story of the CIA's Secret Airlines*. Avon Books republished this riveting saga in the United States in 1985 under a new title, *Air America*.

Other warriors may have seen the childish "action-adventure" motion picture, *Air America*. Supposedly based on the book, the movie degenerated into a satirical farce aimed at legions of teenagers. It was devoid of any semblance of reality.

Many other warriors have heard the whispers and the rumors. Maybe they have listened to the old-timers. Perhaps they have heard tales of getting "sheep-dipped," tales of somehow exchanging the military uniform for civilian clothes to fight for freedom abroad. Where does the truth lie?

The facts: At one time Air America was the largest "airline" in the entire world. The most aircraft. Unlimited finances. *Black Ops*. And the American CIA called all of the shots.

First, a little background is necessary. Prior to World War II, Japan invaded hapless China. Desperate to stop the Japanese, the American government sent Claire L. Chennault and his "American Volunteer Group" to China. These *civilian volunteers*, the famous "Flying Tigers," flew their P-40 fighters against the Japanese Air Force during the struggle for the Chinese mainland.

After World War II ended in 1945, America gave clandestine support to Generalissimo Chiang Kai-Shek in his new battle against the communists. Using the framework of the American Volunteer Group, the American government formed Civil Air Transport (CAT) in 1947. CAT operated a fleet of airplanes to support the war machine of the Chinese Nationalists.

CAT moved its headquarters to the island fortress of Taiwan in 1950 after Free China set up its government there. CAT also began flying regular passenger routes to Tokyo, Bangkok, Manila, and locations throughout the Far East. During the Korean War the men and aircraft of CAT flew a host of clandestine missions that will never find their way into American history books.

The shadowy CAT was "obtained" by the Central Intelligence Agency (CIA) after the Korean War. Flying as Southern Air Transport, Civil Air Transport, Air America, and Air Asia Ltd., the "airline" operated at the direction of the CIA in the western Pacific and in Asia throughout the 1950s.

When the French were on the ropes in Indochina and the American military could not officially intervene, Air America took over. Its mercenaries repeatedly roared into the firestorm at Dien Bien Phu. For public consumption the aircraft and mercenaries never existed; yet, the secrets trickled out. In his acclaimed *Hell in a Very Small Place*, Dr. Bernard B. Fall explained:

> Twenty-four of the twenty-nine C-119s flying as part of the French supply operations had American crews under contract to the Taiwan-based Civil Air Transport.

When the war in Cambodia, Laos, and Vietnam heated up in the 1960s, the CIA consolidated its "airlines" under the name of Air America. The CIA recruited some of its pilots and cargo-kickers from civilian sources, but most of the CIA's mercenary airmen came from the U.S. Armed Forces. Air America made it patently clear whom they wanted: "The most highly skilled, adventurous, and patriotic aviation personnel who could be found."

Aggressive military pilots and aircrewmen of that era had the opportunity to apply for reassignment to Air America. Those who were accepted got "sheep-dipped" and vanished. When next seen, they would be "civilians" flying meticulously maintained silver airplanes and helicopters in Asia. In small black letters on the fuselage of each aircraft were the words, "Air America."

The motto of Air America was simple: "Anything, Anytime, Anywhere." *Rice* was rice. *Hard rice* was ammo. *SAR* was an easy way to get yourself killed in Cambodia, Laos, China, North Vietnam, South Vietnam, or wherever. It did not matter. When you do not officially exist, there are no restrictions.

Most of the former military sheep-dipped pilots and aircrewmen survived. They surfaced years later, mysteriously popping back up in the Marine Corps, Navy, Air Force, Army, or wherever they had vanished from. No questions, no comments.

For the United States, the war in Indochina ended in 1975. Air America more or less disbanded. In *retirement* the mercenary patriots formed the Air America Club. Official recognition, which had never existed, would come 12 years later.

The Air America Memorial now stands at the McDermott Library at the University of Texas in Dallas. It was dedicated on 30 May 1987 by William E. Colby, former Director of the CIA. He titled his emotional dedication address, "Courage in Civilian Clothes." Beginning alphabetically with the name Robert P. Abrams, the bronze memorial lists each of the 242 *civilians* who lost their lives with Air America. The inscription begins:

> This memorial is dedicated to the aircrews and ground support personnel of Civil Air Transport, Air America, Air Asia, and Southern Air Transport, who died while serving the cause of freedom in Asia from 1947 to 1975 . . . .

William P. Clements Jr., Governor of Texas, offered his greetings to the hundreds of Air America survivors who attended. He wrote: "It is high time that these brave individuals be honored." Although Ronald Reagan, President of the United States, was not present, he sent a personal letter on White House stationery:

> . . . Unsung and unrecognized, each of you confronted danger and endured terrible hardships, and each of you rose to the challenge; you never faltered. Although free people everywhere owe you more than we can hope to repay, our greatest debt is to your companions who gave their last full measure of devotion. Just as their names are inscribed on this memorial, so their memories are inscribed in our hearts . . . God bless you, and God bless America.

Has the CIA's airline, by whatever name, *really* faded away? The United States' intelligence community remains on the job.

Somewhere in the world there is always a challenge for American adventurers, warriors, and patriots. In the "Introduction" to his book, *The Invisible Air Force: The True Story of the CIA's Secret Airlines*, author Christopher Robbins notes:

> Air America is a company incorporated in Delaware, but it is also a generic name used to describe all of the CIA air activities . . . There is a web of dozens of CIA airlines throughout the world which should perhaps go under the title, CIA AIR. But, that is a logo you will not find anywhere.

In the mid-1980s in Nicaragua, Contra rebels battled the ruling Sandinistas. On 5 October 1986 the Sandinistas managed to shoot down a shadowy arms-carrying supply plane. Aircraft documents found at the crash site revealed that the plane was owned by Southern Air Transport (sound familiar?). The pilot, William Cooper, and the copilot, Wallace "Buzz" Sawyer, were killed. The only surviving crewmember turned out to be a U.S. Marine Corps veteran, Eugene Hausenfauss. Another U.S. Marine, the gung-ho Col. Oliver North, eventually took the "Contra" flak and the fall and became a highly visible American hero.

So, does Air America still live today? (No problem, just review public listings of charter air carriers.) In the ongoing battle against terrorism and tyranny, can America continue to rely on her *civilian* warriors? (Hint: it's a no-brainer.)

> Americans love to fight. All red-blooded Americans love the sting and clash of battle.
> [Gen. George S. Patton Jr., USA; speaking to the soldiers of his Third Army, in England, 5 June 1944]

Two Days of Honor, and a Place to Remember

-- Memorial Day --

The United States observed the first *Decoration Day* on 30 May 1868, three years after the end of the American Civil War. Gen. John A. Logan, USA, commander of the Grand Army of the Republic, started this annual day of remembrance. He ordered soldiers at U.S. Army posts to decorate the graves of fallen Civil War comrades with flowers and a "suitable ceremony." The order also required that all flags be flown at half mast until noon.

Decoration Day later got a new name, Memorial Day. On this day the nation now honors those killed-in-action from all branches of the U.S. Armed Forces. This day of honor has been further expanded to include all wars and conflicts in which American Warriors have made the Supreme Sacrifice for their country.

Since the late 1950s on the Thursday before Memorial Day, the U.S. Army has placed small American flags at each of the quarter-million-plus graves in Arlington National Cemetery. The Army also stands guard in the cemetery through Memorial Day to make sure that no one disturbs the flags.

In 1968 (the height of the hippie and flower-power generation), Congress changed the observance date from 30 May to the last Monday in May. However, in 1999, bills were introduced in both the House of Representatives and the Senate, proposing restoration of 30 May as the day of observance.

According to tradition, Memorial Day is observed by placing flowers or small flags on the graves of American Warriors who have fallen in battle. Citizens are encouraged to visit military memorials and to fly flags at half mast until noon. They also are asked to fly the relatively new "POW/MIA" flag per the 1998 Defense Authorization Act. Moreover, all Americans are asked to participate in a "Moment of Remembrance" at 3:00 pm and pledge to aid the families of the honored dead.

In many of the southern states, in addition to the national Memorial Day, citizens also observe Confederate Memorial Day. On this day they honor the Confederate soldiers, sailors, and Marines who died in battle during the American Civil War, 1861-1865. Because Confederate Memorial Day is an individual *state* holiday, each state may select its day of observance. Confederate Memorial Day is observed in Florida, Georgia, and Mississippi on April 26; in South Carolina and North Carolina on May 10; and in Alabama on the last Monday in April. It is observed in Virginia on May 30; in Kentucky, Tennessee, and Louisiana on June 3 (the birthday of Jefferson Davis, CSA President); and in Texas on January 19 (the birthday of Gen. Robert E. Lee, CSA).

-- Veterans Day --

After four years of carnage in Europe, the giant cannons finally fell silent. At 11:00 am on 11 November (the 11th hour, of the 11th day, of the 11th month) 1918, the Allies and Germany signed an armistice. The Great War, The World War, The War to End War, mercifully came to an end.

The whole western world rejoiced. Thereafter the eleventh day of November became *Armistice Day* in most nations of the world. In Canada it became known as *Remembrance Day*. In the United States, Congress officially recognized Armistice Day in 1926. Twelve years later, 11 November was declared a national holiday.

Three decades and two wars later, America realized that world order had been equally preserved by veterans of World War II and the Korean War. Consequently, in 1954, Dwight D. Eisenhower, U.S. President, signed legislation that changed the name of Armistice Day to Veterans Day.

In 1968 (the flower-power generation was hard at work again), Congress changed the day of observance to the fourth Monday in October. Veterans Day had temporarily become just another long three-day weekend. Therefore, the reason for the holiday was soon forgotten by many.

Fortunately the public outcry rose steadily over the next ten years. Finally bowing to public pressure, Congress reversed itself in 1978.

The eleventh day of November again became the day on which Americans observe Veterans Day.

By law, Veterans Day is set aside to honor our nation's military veterans, both living and dead, who served in the U.S. Armed Forces in time of war. The focal point for national observance is the Tomb of the Unknown Soldier, often called the Tomb of the Unknowns, in Arlington National Cemetery. At 11:00 am on 11 November, a color guard that includes all four military services executes "Present Arms." The President of the United States lays a wreath upon the tomb, steps back, and salutes. A bugler plays *Taps*. A grateful nation has not forgotten.

-- Tomb of the Unknown Soldier --

After World War I ground to a merciful end, Rev. David Railton visited a military cemetery in France. There he knelt beside the graves of hundreds of British soldiers who had been killed in battle during The War to End War. Rev. Railton noted a grave marked only by a wooden cross. Upon the small cross was handwritten: "An unknown British soldier of the Black Watch."

Rev. Railton proposed that the unidentified soldier be brought home to England. The British government agreed, and the project took on a life of its own. Amid much ceremony the soldier was disinterred in France. With full military honors he was returned to England and laid to rest in Westminster Abbey on 11 November 1920. The state memorial service included an honor guard of British soldiers who had been awarded the Victoria Cross, England's highest award for valor. The tomb inscription reads:

A British Soldier Who Fell In The Great War 1914-1918
For King And Country

Another such gesture of honor took place in France. An unidentified French soldier who had been killed in The Great War was reinterred at the Arc de Triomphe.

The commanding general of American forces in France learned of these projects while they were still in the planning stages. He proposed a similar American plan to the U.S. Army Chief of Staff. The United States approved the reinterrment of an "American unknown soldier" during the 66th Congress on 4 March 1921.

The remains of an unidentified American combattant (there were hundreds from which to choose) were disinterred in France. On 11 November 1921, then *Armistice Day*, the mortal remains of this American Patriot entered their final resting place, a marble tomb on the Plaza of the Memorial Amphitheater in Arlington National Cemetery. The tomb is inscribed with these words:

Here Rests In Honored Glory An American Soldier
Known But To God

On Memorial Day in 1958, two more unidentified American war dead were interred at the tomb. One had been killed in World War II, and the other had sacrificed his life in the service of his country during the war in Korea.

Twenty-six years later in 1984, an unidentified American killed during the war in Vietnam was interred beside the others. He would remain there only 14 years. Because of DNA analysis and other new identification techniques, this warrior was eventually identified as Lt. Michael Blassie, USAF. In 1998 his family chose to remove his remains and bury them elsewhere.

Today the Tomb of the Unknown Soldier is often called the Tomb of the Unknowns. Here the interred unidentified American combatants now represent all of the missing and unidentified warriors who have fallen in battle in the service of their country. Many families whose son, father, uncle, husband, or brother never returned home from conflict abroad make frequent visits to the Tomb of the Unknown Soldier.

Since 1937 the tomb has been guarded 24 hours per day by "The Old Guard," the ceremonial 3rd Army Infantry. Inclusion in this elite unit is one of the highest honors the U.S. Army can bestow upon a soldier. The ritual "changing of the guard" each hour during the day, and each two hours at night, is among the most solemn military ceremonies in the United States.

Code of Conduct
and
General Orders

-- Code of Conduct --

During the Korean War in the early 1950s, the Chinese Army and North Korean Army captured some American military men. These American prisoners then faced a deadly new enemy, the *Eastern World's* POW environment.

For the American prisoners, brutal torture, random genocide, lack of food, absence of medical aid, and subhuman treatment became the daily norm. Many of the Americans found that their training had not prepared them for this *new battlefield*.

After the war the American Armed Forces jointly developed a Code of Conduct. The President of the United States approved this written code in 1955. The six articles of the code constitute a comprehensive guide for all American military forces in time of war, and in time of peace. The articles of the code embrace (1) general statements of dedication to the United States and to the cause of freedom, (2) conduct on the battlefield, and (3) conduct as a prisoner of war.

The Code of Conduct is not a part of the Uniform Code of Military Justice (UCMJ). Instead, the Code of Conduct constitutes a personal action mandate for members of the American Armed Forces throughout the world:

Article I: I am an American, fighting in the armed forces which guard my country and our way of life. I am prepared to give my life in their defense.

Article II: I will never surrender of my own free will. If in command I will never surrender the members of my command while they still have the means to resist.

Article III: If I am captured, I will continue to resist by all means available. I will make every effort to escape and aid others to escape. I will accept neither parole nor special favors from the enemy.

Article IV: If I become a prisoner of war, I will keep faith with my fellow prisoners. I will give no information nor take part in any action which might be harmful to my comrades. If I am senior, I will take command. If not, I will obey the lawful orders of those appointed over me and will back them up in every way.

Article V: When questioned, should I become a prisoner of war, I am required to give name, rank, service number, and date of birth. I will evade answering further questions to the utmost of my ability. I will make no oral or written statements disloyal to my country and its allies or harmful to their cause.

Article VI: I will never forget that I am an American, responsible for my actions, and dedicated to the principles which made my country free. I will trust in my God and in the United States of America.

-- General Orders --

The General Orders for American Armed Forces do not change. They constitute the unyielding bedrock upon which sentries on "guard duty" enforce military security in the United States and throughout the world. General Orders dictate the conduct of all American Warriors on guard duty. These orders apply at all bases and outposts in time of peace, and in time of war.

Recruits in basic training must memorize these General Orders. Woe be unto the unfortunate trainee who can not shout out, verbatim and without hesitation, all of them. Such a recruit will incur a firestorm of wrath from his superiors. There is sound logic for this rigid training. The General Orders will guide each warrior throughout his years of service in the U.S. Armed Forces:

United States Army: The Army keeps directives for its sentries general in nature, preferring to rely on Special Orders to fill in necessary details and instructions. There are only three General Orders for soldiers, as follows:

1.   I will guard everything within the limits of my post and quit my post only when properly relieved.

2.   I will obey my special orders and perform all of my duties in a military manner.

3.   I will report violations of my special orders, emergencies, and anything not covered in my instructions to the commander of the relief.

United States Navy: The Navy has given its sentries eleven General Orders (which are almost identical to those used by the Marine Corps). These General Orders are listed below:

1.   To take charge of this post and all government property in view.

2.   To walk my post in a military manner, keeping always on the alert, and observing everything that takes place within sight or hearing.

3.   To report all violations of orders I am instructed to enforce.

4.   To repeat all calls from posts more distant from the guard house than my own.

5.   To quit my post only when properly relieved.

6.   To receive, obey, and pass on to the sentry who relieves me all orders from the commanding officer, command duty officer, officer of the deck, and officers and petty officers of the watch only.

7.   To talk to no one except in line of duty.

8. To give the alarm in case of fire or disorder.

9. To call the officer of the deck in any case not covered by instructions.

10. To salute all officers and all colors and standards not cased.

11. To be especially watchful at night, and, during the time for challenging, to challenge all persons on or near my post and to allow no one to pass without proper authority.

United States Marine Corps: The origin of the General Orders for U.S. Marines on guard duty has been misplaced in the fog of history. The Marine Corps is a part of the Department of the Navy, and the General Orders used by Marines are almost identical to those used by Navy sailors. Perhaps the Marines originated the General Orders, and the Navy later adopted them. Or, maybe it was the other way around.

The only difference between the General Orders for the Navy and those for the Marine Corps is a minor wording nuance due to the terminology used by the two military services. Like the Navy, the Marine Corps has eleven General Orders. The slightly different wording of General Order No. 6 and General Order No. 9 follows:

6. To receive, obey, and pass on to the sentry who relieves me all orders from the commanding officer, officer of the day, and officers and noncommissioned officers of the guard only.

9. To call the corporal of the guard in any case not covered by instructions.

United States Air Force: The Air Force uses specialized security units on its bases. Previously called *Security Police* and later *Air Police*, the Air Force Security Forces provide guard duty functions, access control, law enforcement, and military security. These Security Forces have three basic General Orders:

1. I will take charge of my post and protect all personnel and property for which I am assigned until properly relieved.

2. I will report all violations of instructions which I am required to enforce and contact my supervisor in those cases not covered by instruction.

3. I will sound the alarm in case of disturbance or emergency.

> In this century, hundreds of thousands of G.I.s died to bring to the beginning of the 21st Century the victory of democracy as the ascendant political system on the face of the Earth. The G.I.s were willing to travel far away and give their lives, if necessary, to secure the rights and freedoms of others . . . All they asked for in repayment from those they freed was the opportunity to help them become part of the world of democracy -- and just enough land to bury their fallen comrades, beneath simple white crosses and Stars of David.
>
> The volunteer G.I.s of today stand watch in Korea, the Persian Gulf, Europe, and the dangerous terrain of the Balkans. We must never see them as mere hirelings, off in a corner of our society. They are our best, and we owe them our full support and our sincerest thanks.
>
> [Gen. Colin Powell, USA, also U.S. Secretary of State; in an essay reprinted in *USAA Magazine*, June 2000]

Somber Reflections on Combat

First, a few somber lines to set the stage:

> God of our fathers, known of old,
>   Lord of our far-flung battle line,
> Beneath whose awful hand we hold
>   Dominion over palm and pine --
> Lord God of Hosts, be with us yet,
> Lest we forget -- lest we forget!
>   [Rudyard Kipling, *Recessional*, 1897]

Warfare and history can not be separated. In a sense, the history of mankind *is* the history of war. Those who have tasted combat know that war is obscene, terrible beyond mortal description.

Yet, throughout the centuries war has remained with us. St. Matthew reminds us that there will be "wars and rumours of wars" and that "nation shall rise against nation, and kingdom against kingdom . . . ." The history books have proved St. Matthew to be correct. Some nations resort to warfare out of need or greed or religious fervor. Other countries take up arms in self defense, to battle terrorism and tyranny, or to thwart assorted evils.

Historically the individual soldiers, the warriors, the centurions, the legionnaires, the individual combatants, have come from the ranks of the common man. Bound together by unity of cause and dedication to their brothers-in-arms, they are revered by their countrymen. For these warriors, warfare rarely brings fame and glory. Most of the time, warfare brings misery, privation, grief, agony, and indiscriminate death. War's toll is horror, hardship, cruelty, and madness.

The following words, arranged in chronological order, come from men who have seen the face of war. Fame and glory are fleeting. Combat is ugly, obscene, and insane. For the individual warrior, often the only victory that remains is eternal loyalty to his fellow brothers-in-arms, his friends for life:

War is sweet to those who have never experienced it.
  [Pindar (522-443 BC), Greek poet]

Go tell the Spartans, thou that passeth by,
That here, obedient to the laws, we lie.
  [epitaph for the Spartan soldiers who fell in battle while holding
  the pass at Thermopylae, 480 BC]

Only the dead have seen the end òf war.
  [Plato (428-347 BC), Greek philosopher]

I did not mean to be killed today.
  [Vicomte de Turenne, a wounded French soldier; as he lay dying
  after the Battle of Salzbach, 1675]

These are the times that try men's souls. The summer soldier and
the sunshine patriot will, in this crisis, shrink from the service of
their country . . . Tyranny, like hell, is not easily conquered.
  [Thomas Paine, *The American Crisis*, 1776]

War is a rough, violent trade.
  [Johann C. Schiller, *The Piccolomini*, 1799]

Thank God I have done my duty.
  [the dying words of Viscount Horatio Nelson, RN; wounded
  aboard his *HMS Victory* off Cape Trafalgar, 21 October 1805]

On fame's eternal camping ground
Their silent tents are spread,
And glory guards with solemn round
The bivouac of the dead.
  [Theodore O'Hara, *The Bivouac of the Dead*, 1847 (by an
  Act of Congress, to be displayed in every National Cemetery)]

Theirs not to make reply,
Theirs not to reason why,
Theirs but to do and die.
Into the valley of Death rode the six hundred.
  [Alfred Tennyson, *The Charge of the Light Brigade*, 1854]

If a man had told me twelve months ago that men could stand such hardships, I would have called him a fool.
[Lt. James H. Langhorne, CSA; 8 January 1862]

Why does Colonel Grigsby refer to me to learn how to deal with mutineers? He should shoot them where they stand.
[LtGen. Thomas J. "Stonewall" Jackson, CSA; in regard to requests for discharge from 12-month volunteers, May 1862]

No tongue can tell, no mind can conceive, no pen can portray, the horrible sights I witnessed this morning.
[Capt. John Taggart, USA; South Mountain, 17 September 1862]

Remember that the enemy you engage have no feelings of kindness or mercy towards you.
[MGen. Thomas C. Hindman, CSA; 7 December 1862]

It is well that war is so terrible -- we would grow too fond of it.
[Gen. Robert E. Lee, CSA; Fredericksburg, 13 December 1862]

Major, tell my father I died with my face to the enemy.
[Col. Issac E. Avery, CSA; his last words, spoken to his adjutant as he lay mortally wounded at Gettysburg, 2 July 1863]

Well, general, let's bury these poor men and say no more about it.
[Gen. Robert E. Lee, CSA; to MGen. A.P. Hill, CSA; in regard to the Confederate dead at Briscoe Station, 14 October 1863]

. . . We cannot dedicate, we cannot consecrate, we cannot hallow this ground. The brave men, living and dead, who struggled here have consecrated it far above our poor power to add or detract. The world will little note, nor long remember what we say here, but it can never forget what they did here.
[Abraham Lincoln, U.S. President; dedicating the National Cemetery at Gettysburg battlefield, 19 November 1863]

Don't worry. They couldn't hit an elephant at this dist . . . .
[the last words of Gen. John Sedgwick, USA; standing atop the parapet to direct artillery fire, and speaking to an aide who was

pleading with him to take cover, just as he was shot through the neck and killed by a CSA sniper at Spotsylvania, 8 May 1864]

I had rather die than be whipped.
[MGen. J.E.B. "Jeb" Stuart, CSA; to his staff after he fell, mortally wounded, at Yellow Tavern, 11 May 1864]

War is cruelty and you cannot refine it.
[Gen. William T. Sherman, USA; in a letter to the Mayor of Atlanta, 12 September 1864]

None can realize the horrors of war, save those actually engaged. The dead lying all about, unburied to the last. My God! My God! What a scourge is war!
[Samuel Johnson, Sixth Georgia, CSA; in a letter to his family]

When I was taken prisoner I weighed 165 pounds, and when I came out I weighed 96 pounds, and was considered stout compared to many I saw there.
[Pvt. A.S. Clyne, USA; a former POW at Andersonville]

There's only one truth about war: people die.
[Gen. Philip H. Sheridan (1831-1888), USA]

Not for fame or reward, not for place or rank,
Not lured by ambition or goaded by necessity;
But in simple obedience to duty as they understood it,
These men suffered all, sacrificed all,
Dared all - and died.
[a eulogy by Rev. Randolph H. McKim, CSA chaplain; inscribed on the Confederate Memorial in Arlington National Cemetery]

There is many a boy here today who looks on war as all glory. But, boys, war is Hell! . . . It is only those who have neither fired a shot nor heard the shrieks and groans of the wounded who cry aloud for blood, more vengeance, more destruction.
[Gen. William T. Sherman, USA; addressing a patriotic gathering of military veterans and young men, 12 August 1880]

War loses a great deal of its romance after a soldier has seen his first battle.
[Col. John Mosby, CSA; *Mosby's War Reminiscences*, 1887]

Don't cheer, men. The poor devils are dying.
[Capt. John W. Philip, USN; as his *USS Texas* passed the burning Spanish warship *Vizcaya* at Santiago, Cuba, 3 July 1898]

If I come out of this war alive, I will have more luck than brains.
[Baron Capt. Manfred von Richthofen (The Red Baron), German Flying Service; in a letter to his mother, 1914]

I have seen war, and faced modern artillery, and I know what an outrage it is against simple men.
[Thomas M. Kettle, *The Ways of War*, 1915]

The effects of the successful gas attack were horrible. I am not pleased with the idea of poisoning men. Of course the entire world will rage about it at first -- and then imitate us.
[Rudolph Binding, *A Fatalist at War*, 1915, in regard to the German use of lethal gas at Vijfwege, Belgium, in April 1915]

With a bullet through his head, he fell from an altitude of 9000 feet, a beautiful death.
[Baron Capt. Manfred von Richthofen (The Red Baron), German Flying Service; in a letter describing the death of his friend, Count von Holck, near Verdun, France, 1 May 1916]

My God! Did we really send men to fight in that?
[LtGen. Sir Launcelot E. Kiggell, British Army; upon seeing the mud and carnage after the Battle of Passchendaele, 1917]

What's the matter? Do you think that perhaps I will not return?
[Baron Capt. Manfred von Richthofen (The Red Baron), German Flying Service; speaking to the airplane mechanic who asked for his autograph before his final and fatal flight, 21 April 1918]

I have seen blood running from the wounded. I have seen men coughing out their gassed lungs. I have seen the dead in the mud.

I have seen two hundred limping, exhausted men come out of the line -- the survivors of a regiment of one thousand that went forward forty-eight hours before.
[Franklin D. Roosevelt, Assistant Secretary of the Navy (later U.S. President); in Belleau Wood, France, June 1918]

I have only two men out of my company and 20 out of some other company. We need support, but it is almost suicide to try to get it here as we are swept by machine gun fire and a constant barrage is on us. I have no one on my left and only a few on my right. I will hold.
[1stLt. Clifton B. Cates, USMC; in France, 19 July 1918]

War would end if the dead could return.
[Stanley Baldwin (1867-1947), British Prime Minister]

War, like any other racket, pays high dividends to the very few.
[MGen. Smedley D. Butler, USMC; 1933]

Enemy on island. Issue in doubt.
[last radio transmission from the besieged American garrison on Wake Island, 23 December 1941]

Every day kill just one, rather than today five, tomorrow ten. Then your nerves are calm and you can sleep good. You have your drink in the evening and the next morning you are fit again.
[Col. Erich Hartmann, Luftwaffe; 352 air-to-air kills, WW II]

Older men declare war. But it is youth that must fight and die.
[Herbert Hoover, former U.S. President; 27 June 1944]

The beach was a sheet of flame backed by a wall of black smoke, as though the island was on fire . . . We piled out of our Amtrac amid blue-white Japanese machine gun tracers and raced inland.
[PFC Eugene B. Sledge, USMC; Peleliu, 15 September 1944]

Such a sight on that beach! Wrecked boats, bogged down jeeps, tanks burning, casualties scattered all over!
[Michael Kelecher, USN surgeon; Iwo Jima, February 1945]

All I wanted to get out of Iwo Jima was my fanny and dog tags.
  [Cpl. Edward Hartman, USMC; after the battle, March 1945]

How can I feel like a hero, when I hit the beach with two-hundred
and fifty buddies, and only twenty-seven of us walked off alive?
  [PFC Ira A. Hayes, USMC; speaking on 16 April 1945 in reply
  to a remark about his role in raising the American flag atop Mt.
  Suribachi, Iwo Jima, on 23 February 1945]

You never knew when you were drawing your last breath. You
lived in total uncertainty, on the brink of the abyss, day after day.
  [PFC Eugene B. Sledge, USMC; Okinawa, 1945]

Another improvement was that we built our gas chambers to
accommodate two thousand people at one time.
  [Rudolf Hess (1894-1987), Deputy Fuhrer of Nazi Germany;
  during his imprisonment after World War II]

A million deaths is a mere statistic.
  [Josef W. Stalin (1879-1953), Russian dictator]

Consider yourselves already dead. Once you accept that idea, it
won't be so tough.
  [the fictitious World War II leader, Gen. Frank Savage, U.S.
  Army Air Corps; portrayed by Gregory Peck in the motion
  picture, *Twelve O'Clock High*, 1949]

The experience helped me realize how fragile life is. There could
be two of you standing there . . . and in the next minute, only one.
  [Pvt. Jack McCorkle, USMC; 23 March 2001, speaking of the
  fighting at Chosin Reservoir, Korea, in December 1950]

The staff intelligence officer handed me the pre-strike photos, the
coordinates of the target, and told me to get on with it. He didn't
mention that the bridges were defended by 56 radar-controlled
antiaircraft guns.
  [Capt. Paul N. Gray, USN; speaking years later of attacking the
  bridges at Toko-ri, Korea, on 12 December 1951]

The situation of the wounded is particularly tragic. They are piled on top of each other in holes that are completely filled with mud and devoid of any hygiene.

[Bernard B. Fall, *Hell in a Very Small Place*, 1966, quoting a French Army radio message from Dien Bien Phu, 5 May 1954]

The Legionnaire next to me disintegrated. Nothing was left of him except little pieces of raw meat. Death was spitting all around us. Men were falling like flies.

[a survivor of Dien Bien Phu in 1954; speaking years later]

The wounded were still lying there just like on the first day, intermingled with men who had died several days ago and were beginning to rot. They were lying there unattended, in the tropical sun, being eaten alive by the rats and the vultures. If only they had all been dead! *[and also]* As night fell over Dien Bien Phu the Legionnaires fixed bayonets in the ghostly light of the parachute flares and -- 600 against 40,000 -- walked into death.

[Bernard B. Fall, *Street Without Joy*, 1961]

The survivors would envy the dead.

[Nikita Khruschev, Premier of the Soviet Union; speaking of the possibility of global nuclear war, 1962]

By that time every Marine had been wounded. The living took the ammunition of the dead and lay under a moonless sky, wondering about the next assault.

[Capt. Francis J. West Jr., USMC; writing of combat on 13 June 1966 in *Small Unit Action in Vietnam, Summer 1966*]

We were being attacked by a thousand men. We just couldn't kill them fast enough.

[Sgt. John J. McGinty, USMC; speaking of combat on 18 July 1966 in *U.S. Marines in Vietnam, an Expanding War, 1966*]

One [survivor was] about eighteen, covered with gunpowder and dirt, black under the eyes. They were glassy. He was exhausted. Man, he looked bad, real bad. He said he had his bayonet fixed all night. I asked him if he had been scared, and he said, "Yeah."

Right before daylight he had one bullet left. *One* bullet, just *one* bullet. So he started throwing rocks at the [enemy] in the dark. You know, tryin' to make 'em think the rocks were grenades. Only *one* bullet left. He was saving it for the final charge. He told me he realized he was gonna' die. Then, once he accepted that, he wasn't scared anymore.
    [Capt. William T. Holmes, USMC; referencing a conversation in Vietnam on 9 August 1966, quoted in *Bonnie-Sue*, 1996]

He charged a machine gun bunker with hand grenades, trying to save some guys. He didn't have to do it. He got slaughtered. He had two kids.
    [Capt. Otto H. Fritz, USMC; speaking years later of a sergeant in his company in Vietnam, October 1966]

Two machine guns keep up intense fire. NVA now have us almost surrounded. I have a terrible feeling I will never see my family again . . . Air strikes coming every 30 seconds. The ground trembles continuously. Once again I feel the end is near -- at least for me. I get an uncontrollable case of the shakes. I wonder if I ever had what it takes to be a Marine and conclude that I never did and don't now.
    [Arnaud de Borchgrave, combat correspondent; "The Battle for Hill 400," in *Newsweek*, 10 October 1966]

Otto, you go ahead. I'm a dead man.
    [1stLt. Steve Sayer, USMC; to his friend, 1stLt. Otto Fritz, the moment before Sayer was KIA in Vietnam, 10 December 1966]

Mike Company ceased to exist on that day; out of 190 men, only 26 were left standing.
    [Austin Deuel, in *Vietnam Magazine*, describing 30 April 1967]

Where are those [expletive] choppers? All of my emergency medevacs are dead! All my priorities are now emergencies!
    [HM3 Thomas Lindenmeyer, USN; Vietnam, 2 July 1967]

I don't think I'll be talking to you again. We are being overrun.
    [the last radio message from Capt. Warren O. Keneipp, USMC;

his body, staked out and decapitated, was found 5 July 1967]

He was blown in half for a [expletive] place that had no strategic value, no military value, no sense to it, save to prove to Russia or China or North Vietnam or God or somebody that nineteen year old low and middle-class Americans would die for their country.
   [a teenage U.S. Marine at Con Thien, Vietnam, 1967]

He was burning to death in the plane and couldn't get out. He was [screaming for] someone to tell his wife that he loved her, and for someone to shoot him.
   [Chaplain Ray Stubbe, USN; *The Final Formation*, 1995, quoting a witness to the death of a pilot at Khe Sanh on 23 August 1967]

We found part of Scribner's helmet with part of his head still inside . . . [it] looked like the rocket went off right in his lap. There was nothing left.
   [Chaplain Ray Stubbe, USN; *The Final Formation*, 1995, quoting a warrior speaking of the death of a friend on 24 January 1968]

We huddled together in the bunker, shoulders high and necks pulled in to leave no space between helmet and flak jacket. There is no describing an artillery barrage. The earth shakes, clods of dirt fall from the ceiling, and shrapnel makes a repulsive singing through the air.
   [John Donnelly, combat correspondent; "Drawing the Noose" at Khe Sanh, in *Newsweek*, 5 February 1968]

Everything I see is blown through with smoke, everything is on fire everywhere. It doesn't matter that memory distorts; every image, every sound comes back out of smoke and the smell of things burning. *[and also]* The Grunts themselves knew: the madness, bitterness, the horror and doom of it. *[and also]* The belief that one Marine was better than ten Slopes saw Marine squads fed in against known NVA platoons, platoons against companies, and on and on, until whole battalions found themselves pinned down and cut off. That belief was undying, but the Grunt was not.
   [Michael Herr, *Dispatches*, 1968]

Sometimes in the morning we'd see three or four hundred bodies out along the wire. *[and also]* Every inch of the runway was zeroed in, and if an airplane tried to land they just walked artillery rounds right up the center line. *[and also]* They had the glide slope zeroed in with .50 caliber machine guns and they knew exactly where to shoot to hit you on it. They'd just listen for you and start laying fire down the glide slope. If you were on it, you were drilled.
[LtCol. David L. Althoff, USMC; in "Helicopter Operations at Khe Sanh," *Marine Corps Gazette*, May 1969]

It was raining. I was a replacement for a company commander who had been killed the night before. The tank lurched to a halt. I jumped off, walked over to a hole and asked, "Where is the CP?" A filthy, soaking wet Marine continued bailing out his hole with a C-ration can and answered, "You're in it." I asked for the battalion commander. He answered, "You're looking at him."
[Maj. M.P. Caulfield, USMC; writing of combat near Con Thien, Vietnam, in "India Six," *Marine Corps Gazette*, July 1969]

(1) There was no conversation, just heavy grunting as they beat him with their fists . . . there was a steady "thump, thump." The guards had become more agitated and were beating his head against his wooden pallet. *[and also]* (2) Jerry, I'm in bad shape. They are giving me almost nothing to eat. I'm down to a hundred pounds and I haven't crapped in twenty-six days. I don't remember how long I've been in irons, but it's been weeks. I don't know whether I can make it.
[RAdm. Jeremiah A. Denton Jr., USN (later a U.S. Senator); *When Hell Was in Session*, 1976, (1) describing the beating of a fellow POW, and (2) paraphrasing a fellow POW's words]

Samuels looked down and saw that his left leg was flipped crazily to one side midway down below the knee. There was no way his leg could be lying there like that and still be -- still be attached.
[C.D.B. Bryan, *Friendly Fire*, 1976]

War runs best on evil . . . How else can you convince boys to kill one another day after day? *[and also]* War is not killing. Killing is the easiest part of the whole thing. Sweating twenty-four hours a day, seeing guys drop all around you of heatstroke, not having food, not having water, sleeping only three hours a night for weeks at a time, that's what war is. *[and also]* I'd pray for a firefight, just so we could stop walking.

[Mark Baker, *NAM*, 1981]

It was a slaughter. No better than lining people up on the edge of a ditch and shooting them in the back of the head. I was doing it enthusiastically.

[unidentified helicopter gunner, quoted in *NAM*, 1981]

There was a Christmas truce, but we flew anyway. I couldn't get over how bizarre it was. We would decide to stop killing each other for a few days, and then start again. *[and also]* I felt like a worm on a string. The tracers rushed past us like a line of UFOs in a hurry. I promised God that I would quit smoking and I would never touch a whore, not even get a hand job, and I would believe in Him if He would only let me live.

[WO Robert Mason, USA; *Chickenhawk*, 1984]

The enduring emotion of war, when everything else has faded, is comradeship. A comrade in war is a man you can trust with anything, because you have trusted him with your life. *[and also]* In war the line between life and death is gossamer thin; there is joy, true joy, in being alive when so many around you are not.

[William Broyles Jr., "Why Men Love War," in *Esquire*, 1984]

The POWs I saw were very thin; they were covered with scabies -- there was just skin and bones left on them. They could hardly walk, yet they were forced to carry wood from the forests. They often fell down. They were beaten by the guards.

[unidentified South Vietnamese soldier, in *Life on the Line*, 1988]

The only thing clean borne of this life is cruelty and filth.

[an unidentified British private, quoted in *Eye Deep in Hell: Trench Warfare in World War I*, 1989]

I now know why men who have been to war yearn to reunite. Not

to tell war stories or look at old pictures. Not to laugh or weep. Comrades gather because they long to be with men who once acted their best, men who suffered and sacrificed, who were stripped raw, right down to their humanity. . . I have never given anyone such trust. They were willing to guard something more precious than my life. They would have carried my reputation, the memory of me. It was part of the bargain we all made, the reason we were so willing to die for one another.
[Michael Norman, *These Good Men*, 1990]

Thirty, forty, maybe fifty Marines lay twisted along both sides of the road, clumped atop each other in spots, their weapons and gear strewn down the middle of the road . . . a slaughterhouse.
[William K. Nolan, *Operation Buffalo*, 1991]

Death is so commonplace it doesn't shock you anymore. *[and also]* Flying in the night rain with fog was a death warrant.
[LtCol. H. Lee Bell, USMC; *1369*, 1992]

He was just a kid, as was I. He confided to me that he had never even kissed a girl before . . . Unfortunately, he never got the chance. I think his mother would be happy to know that only God and her [sic] ever knew the tenderness of his kiss.
[Chaplain Ray Stubbe, USN; *The Final Formation*, 1995, quoting a friend of PFC Bruce Cunningham, USMC, KIA in Vietnam]

Our government does not want America to know that our darkest secret is that we killed many Americans in cold blood. They were tortured to death in prison, or simply killed outright from fear they would try to escape. And our leaders are afraid to admit this. They were tortured to death here in Hanoi.
[LtCol. Nguyen Van Thi, Vietnamese Army; in *Inside Hanoi's Secret Archives: Solving the MIA Mystery*, 1995]

We did unspeakable things we won't now admit -- not even to ourselves. We held the God-like power of life and death in our hands. After the war we suppressed the killer instinct, usually hiding it behind a low-key facade of casual humor. But the evil

still lives in us, lurking somewhere just beneath the surface.
[Capt. Marion F. Sturkey, USMC; notes handwritten in 1992 for the "Epilog" of *Bonnie-Sue,* 1996]

War is a cruel game, a brutal game, a deadly game. *[and also]* The overwhelming sensation was that of deafening noise and bedlam. No one could hear the individual weapons firing, the bombs exploding, the shouts and screams. There was only a continuous cacophony, a horrible roar. *[and also]* Low on ammunition, the two wounded Marines crawled among their fallen friends and stripped them of all their remaining grenades and M-16 magazines . . . The alternate radio operator, although unconscious, was still alive. Pulling him between them, they waited, for there was nothing else they could do.
[Capt. Marion F. Sturkey, USMC; *Bonnie-Sue,* 1996]

Men caught in the killing zone became instant dogmeat. *[and also]* Marine helicopter crews who survived an entire tour unscathed led charmed lives. Enemy gunfire downed 1,777 helicopters during the first five years of the war; others returned to base shot to splinters.
[Col. Joseph H. Alexander, USMC; *A Fellowship of Valor,* 1997]

Marines learned the realities of the Western Front: mud, shelling, barbed wire, rats, corpses in various states of disintegration, an almost invisible enemy, trench raids, gas attacks . . . .
[BGen. Edwin H. Simmons, USMC; in *The Marines,* 1998]

Sweat gathered inside our rubber boots, and when we pulled off a sock, frozen skin came with it. Sleep was out of the question. Training enabled us to keep fighting. Surrounded as we were, there was no rear, no front, no flank.
[Sgt. Werner "Ronnie" Reininger, USMC; describing fighting near Hagaru-ri, Korea, in *Leatherneck,* January 2001]

Second place was a body bag.
[Capt. Roger A. Herman, USMC; in *The Log Book,* 2001]

I watched Marines die face down in the mud protecting freedom.
[Col. Oliver North, USMC; 21 September 2001]

-- Points to Ponder --

Labor to keep alive in your breast that little spark of celestial fire called conscience.
[Gen. George Washington (1732-1799), Continental Army; later the first U.S. President]

There was never a time when, in my opinion, some way could not be found to prevent the drawing of the sword.
[Gen. Ulysses S. Grant (1822-1885), USA; also U.S. President]

In wartime, truth is so precious that she should always be attended by a bodyguard of lies.
[Sir Winston Churchill (1874-1965), British Prime Minister]

War to the hilt between communism and capitalism is inevitable. Today, of course, we are not strong enough to attack. Our time will come in twenty to thirty years. To win, we shall need the element of surprise. The bourgeoisie will have to be put to sleep. So we shall begin by launching the most spectacular peace movement on record. There will be electrifying overtures and unheard-of concessions. The capitalist countries, stupid and decadent, will rejoice to cooperate in their own destruction. They will leap at another chance to be friends. As soon as their guard is down, we shall smash them with our clenched fists.
[Dmitri Manuilsky, Lenin School of Political Warfare, 1931]

Although war is evil, it is occasionally the lesser of two evils.
[McGeorge Bundy, student; in an essay at Yale College, 1940]

Beware of war hawks who never served in the military.
[James Bradford, in *USA Today*, 17 September 2002]

The Warriors' Rules for Life

For each American Warrior, life and service constitute a trust, a responsibility, and an opportunity. But before we set out to change the world, we should start at home.

The person we see in the mirror each morning is the person with whom we should begin. The most crucial person with whom we must live is ourselves. In that regard, we must make sure that we remain in good company. If we heed the basic Rules for Life, we will have taken a giant step in that direction:

In matters of *conscience*, ignore the majority.

Dare to be different. If all think alike, none are really thinking.

Shun unanimity when it equates to ethical or moral cowardice.

Right or wrong, your silence equals your consent.

Remember that *character* is what you are in the dark; remember that your *character* is your destiny.

Believe in, and sacrifice for, *a cause greater than self.*

Reject any so-called reasoning which consists of trying to find a basis for believing what you already believe.

Avoid any philosophy supported by an absence of courage.

Remember that (1) small minds discuss people, (2) average minds discuss events, but (3) great minds discuss ideas.

Never wrestle with a pig; never argue with an idiot.

Tilting at windmills hurts you more than it hurts the windmills.

Remember: no monument was ever erected to honor a cynic.

In interpersonal matters, apply the Golden Rule.

It is great to be great. It is *greater* to be human.

Never sneer at anyone's dreams. Dreams may be all they have.

If you always tell the truth, you never have to remember anything.

The better part of your life consists of your friendships.

Never allow a little dispute to injure a great friendship.

Count your wealth by your friends, not your dollars.

Great love, like any great achievement, involves great risk.

Dare to dare. Nothing worthwhile is achieved without risk.

Judge an achievement by what you had to risk to get it.

The greater the potential reward, the greater the guaranteed risk.

Often, not getting what you want may be a fantastic stroke of luck.

The three keys to success: (1) vision (2) initiative (3) commitment.

Never give up, never back down, never give in. Keep scratching.

The path to failure lies in trying to please everyone.

Yesterday is history. Tomorrow is never guaranteed. Today is all that you have to work with.

-- Life is always in session. Are you always present? --

About the Author

Marion Sturkey, a native of the *urban metropolis* of Plum Branch, South Carolina, entered the U.S. Marine Corps in 1961. Seven years later in 1968 he returned to civilian life.

During the next two years, Marion flew commercial helicopters to support the off-shore oil industry in Louisiana and Texas. Thereafter he worked in various management capacities for the BellSouth Corporation for 25 years. During the last ten of those years he served as guest instructor at Bell Communications Research in Illinois and New Jersey. During that time he published his first book, *Gone But Not Forgotten*, a 679 page genealogical monstrosity. He soon followed up with his second book, an abbreviated softcover version.

Leaving the corporate world, Marion researched, authored, and published *BONNIE-SUE: A Marine Corps Helicopter Squadron in Vietnam*, which garnered national acclaim. Reprinted time after time, it remains a classic in both print and audio-book format. Next came *Warrior Culture of the U.S. Marines*, an up-beat look at the world's premier amphibious fighting force.

Today, Marion lives in the idyllic rural community of Plum Branch. *Murphy's Laws of Combat*, his first mainline venture into the military satire genera, is his fifth book.

-- military books by Marion Sturkey --

BONNIE-SUE: A Marine Corps Helicopter Squadron in Vietnam:
(first published in 1996) Professional, 21 photographs, 4 maps, 509
pages. A timeless classic, usually considered the definitive work
on Marine Corps helicopter warfare in Vietnam. Yet, the book
soars high above the mud of war. The author blends emotion,
detail, and grim realism; he breathes life into a daily struggle for
survival. Against the backdrop of the turbulent 1960's era,
BONNIE-SUE' evolves into a riveting true saga of commitment and
sacrifice, love and brotherhood. No profanity.

Warrior Culture of the U.S. Marines: (first published in 2002) 15
photographs, 207 pages. Gung-ho, <u>Politically In-Correct</u> and proud
of it! The book extolls the legendary warrior ethos of the U.S.
Marines, the modern-day American Samurai. It's all here: USMC
quotations, Tun Tavern, the creeds, the War Memorial, the
Commandants, axioms for warriors, and patriot dreams. Also,
blood chit, blood stripe, Corps Values (and much more), plus the
ultimate collection of USMC satire. No profanity.

Murphy's Laws of Combat: (first published in 2003) A walk on
the humorous side of military life. Military satire for all branches
of the U.S. Armed Forces. Hundreds upon hundreds of spirited,
up-beat, and *tongue-in-cheek* Combat Laws, Principles, and
Axioms. Plus, the Warrior's Rules of Sex & Seduction. Also,
historic military quotations, battle legacy, and somber Reflections
on Combat from America's military elite. This is the book for
warriors (or warrior wannabes), young and old, who enjoy a good
laugh -- usually at themselves. No profanity.

Heritage Press International
204 Jefferson Street
P.O. Box 333
Plum Branch, SC 29845
 Phone: 864-443-5081
 Fax: 864-443-5572
 E-Mail: MarionS@wctel.net
 Web Site: www.USMCpress.com

Index

239